Pray
365 Daily Prayers

Presented by

Helen V. Alexander

ISBN-13: 978-1537794273
ISBN-10: 1537794272

Scripture References: KJV/MSG/NIV

www.helenalexanderministries.com
E-mail: hvalexander@yahoo.com

DEDICATION

This book is dedicated to my Pastor, Bishop Arthur L. Jenkins, Sr. He has been a great inspiration in my life. He teaches his flock the importance of having a personal relationship with God! I'm grateful to the Lord to have the opportunity to sit under his leadership.

MISSION STATEMENT

We endeavor to develop, empower, equip and inspire individuals to embrace prayer as the core of their lives.

JANUARY 1

Matthew 21:22

If you believe, you will receive whatever you ask for in prayer.

DECREE FOR TODAY: We decree that today we will be better than yesterday. We will put on a bright color of clothing and walk into that workplace, on the street, and in the home with our minds above what happened yesterday that was not good. God is bigger than that!

Father, in Jesus' Name, thank you for this undeserved grace that you have so freely given to us, whereby we are made spiritually rich! Glory to God! Thank you that through Christ we have access, courage, and boldness to come before the throne of God in confidence by our faith, knowing that you hear us. By faith we receive the riches of your glory which strengthens us with might by your Spirit in our inner man. Thank you, Lord! We will no more be children tossed to and fro and carried about with every wind of doctrine, but we will speak the truth in love so that we may grow up in you, Lord. We will follow on to know you in order that we can mature in you; and having done all, Lord, we will stand because of your power. In Jesus' Name, we thank you!

JANUARY 2

2 Thessalonians 1:3

We ought always to thank God for you, brothers and sisters, and rightly so, because your faith is growing more and more, and the love all of you have for one another is increasing.

DECREE FOR TODAY: We decree that we will hold our peace in the home, on the job, or wherever! Moving without God's direction will result in disaster!

Father, in Jesus' Name, thank you for life. We bless you for the word of God. We will hold fast to righteousness. We are in awe of your power and strength. Your eye seeth every precious thing. Forgive us of our sins and rebellions. Create in us clean hearts and renew a right spirit within us. Thank you for your goodness that is continuous. Thank you for covering us under your wings. You are our shield and buckler. Thank you, Lord, in Jesus' Name!

JANUARY 3

1 Timothy 4:12

Don't let anyone look down on you because you are young, but set an example for the believers in speech, in conduct, in love, in faith and in purity.

DECREE FOR TODAY: We decree that we will take on the "so what" attitude! God is in control of our lives as we yield to him! No weapon formed against us shall prosper.

Father, in Jesus' Name, thank you for grace that woke us up today! Glory to God! Thank you for the power of the Holy Ghost that strengthens your people to endure to the end. Your grace is sufficient for us, Lord. Our strength is made perfect in weakness. We know that all things are working together for our good and our light afflictions are but for a moment. We won't worry about the things that we don't understand, for you have told us not to lean unto our own understanding. Thank you that your ways are not like our ways and your thoughts are not like our thoughts. We will trust in you, Lord, and do good. We will rejoice. We will give you glory. Thank you for making us more than conquerors! Thank you for giving us power to pull down every imagination that is not like you. We say yes to your will. Whatever it is, we say yes! In Jesus' Name, we thank you Lord!

JANUARY 4

John 7:38

Whoever believes in me, as Scripture has said, rivers of living water will flow from within them.

DECREE FOR TODAY: We decree that we will not be harsh with our words, for a soft answer turns away wrath! Let go and let God!

Father, in the Name of Jesus, we thank you for all things. It is a day of gratitude. Thank you for the opportunity to show you some love, Lord! We give you the glory for all that you have done for your people. We are grateful to you, Lord! Thank you for food and the miraculous way that you make it grow, Lord. Thank you for our shelter and transportation. Thank you for jobs, ways, and means; oh, how you open doors and make the impossible become possible. How great is our God! Thank you for the Holy Ghost that enables us to be more than conquerors. Thank you for the mind to think! Glory to God. Lord, how valuable it is for us to be able to think! Thank you for our families. Thank you for the body of Christ.

Thank you that you have provided a way for us to have the Bible. Oh, what a precious gift, Lord! We give you all the glory, in Jesus' Name!

JANUARY 5

Galatians 2:20

I have been crucified with Christ and I no longer live, but Christ lives in me. The life I now live in the body, I live by faith in the Son of God, who loved me and gave himself for me.

DECREE FOR TODAY: We decree that God is our rock and our salvation. He is the rock of our strength!

Father, in Jesus' Name, thank you for the sweetness of your Spirit that comforts us daily, Lord! Your joy is our strength. Your directions lead us in the right paths. Your divine provision for us to keep our minds stayed on you guarantees us perfect peace. Thank you, God! We will delight ourselves in you. We will not forget your word. Open our eyes that we may behold the wondrous things in your word. You have been our help. Through every storm, you have brought us out. Thank you! Our hearts trust in you. We confidently lean on you. We praise you for being our High Tower. Thank you for being our Rock and Strength and a Deliverer in the times of trouble. You gave us life and showed us your unfailing love! You have preserved us and delivered us from the powers of darkness. We are grateful, Lord! In Jesus' Name, we thank you!

JANUARY 6

Hebrews 12:2

Fixing our eyes on Jesus, the pioneer and perfecter of faith. For the joy set before him he endured the cross, scorning its shame, and sat down at the right hand of the throne of God.

DECREE FOR TODAY: We decree that we will allow the glory of the Lord to rise among us! We will ignore distractions and demonic activity taking place around us for God has given us the victory!

Father, in Jesus' Name, thank you for allowing us to dwell in the secret place of the Most High. You are our refuge, our fortress and our God. We will trust in you no matter what we have to endure. You will surely deliver us. Your word is our shield and buckler. We will NOT be afraid of the terror by night nor the arrow that flieth by day in the home, on the job, or wherever! You have given us angels to take charge over us and to keep us in all our ways. You are our ROCK, Lord! You promised to give us an expected end! We wait patiently for the promise. No good thing will you withhold from them that walk uprightly. In Jesus' Name, we thank you!

JANUARY 7

<u>James 2:17</u>

In the same way, faith by itself, if it is not accompanied by action, is dead.

DECREE FOR TODAY: We decree that God's favor is upon us!

Father, in Jesus' Name, thank you for family, people who care, and people that have feelings for others. You are a Mighty God! Nothing is too hard for you! We pray for those that are without family, lonely, pushed to the side, that you will lift them up, Lord. These battles are not ours. They belong to you. You've already made us victorious; we need only to believe it and walk in faith. Every trial is already concluded, and every temptation is already overcome. Calvary took care of it all. Help us not to forget Calvary. Thank you for your Blood that protects; it covers, it heals, and it delivers. It is still as fresh today as it was at Calvary. Thank you, Lord, for the privilege to plead the Blood of Jesus in every situation, in Jesus' Name!

JANUARY 8

<u>Philippians 1:29</u>

"It has been granted to you on behalf of Christ not only to believe in him, but also to suffer for him.

DECREE FOR TODAY: We decree that we will tell God THANK YOU! Thank you for the good times, trials and tribulations.

Father, in Jesus' Name, thank you for mercy! You've spared our lives to see another day! Hallelujah! We believe your word, Lord, for it is impossible to please you without faith. Our faith is not going to stand in the wisdom of men but in the power of God! No height, no depth, no demon, no tribulation, no distress, no persecution, no famine, nothing and nobody will separate us from your love, Lord! We stand firm in your word! We will speak it. We will watch it perform, as you have promised. We thank you for it, in Jesus' Name!

JANUARY 9

<u>Romans 12:3</u>

For by the grace given me I say to every one of you: Do not think of yourself more highly than you ought, but rather think of yourself with sober judgment, in accordance with the faith God has distributed to each of you.

DECREE FOR TODAY: ***We decree that we will shake ourselves from the cares of this world and remind ourselves that Jesus said, in the world we will have much tribulation, but we will be of good cheer because Jesus has overcome the world!***

Father, in Jesus' Name, thank you for your faithfulness. You are the great I AM. You are our Shepherd, our source of supply for all things. We are looking unto the hills from whence cometh our help. God, the world needs you. Oh, it sometimes seems that attention is being focused on everything and everybody but you, God, when you are the answer. Help us to put prayer into the lives of the children. It's a mean world now, Lord, and only your anointing can cover us. Thank you for the assurance that no weapon formed against us shall prosper. It shall not! Thank you, God! Thank you for keeping our bodies as we consume all kinds of foods that may harm or destroy our bodies. Thank you for sifting the air we breathe. Hallelujah! Thank you, in Jesus' Name!

JANUARY 10

<u>Ephesians 2:8-9</u>

For it is by grace you have been saved, through faith—and this is not from yourselves, it is the gift of God—not by works, so that no one can boast.

DECREE FOR TODAY - ***We decree that we will have peace in the mind today no matter what happens. We will keep our minds on God. We will not dwell on our circumstances. God is bigger than that!***

Father, in Jesus' Name, we are grateful to be a part of your creation. Thank you for choosing all of us and making us special people, a royal priesthood, set aside for the Master's use. We won't be troubled by the perilous times and happenings around us. Lord, we will cement ourselves in faith and hope that lies within us. We won't be moved. We will stand against the wiles of the devil having put on the armour that you have given us. We won't be moved by the talk of the day nor the sudden fear that comes to shake us. Oh no, Lord! Our dependence is on you. You are our Rock that is unbreakable. Our strong tower! Our deliver from all afflictions. We rest in you today, casting all of our cares upon you for you care for us. Thank you, Lord, in Jesus' Name!

JANUARY 11

1 John 5:5

Who is it that overcomes the world? Only the one who believes that Jesus is the Son of God.

DECREE FOR TODAY: We decree that we will shake it off!

Father, in Jesus' Name, we thank you for loving us. Zion is calling us to a higher place in you. Glory to God! God, we feel your tug. You're calling your people to that secret place in you. We have to get there, Lord God, so that we can fight the demons of hell. Satan has stepped up. We must go higher. Higher in prayer. Higher in fasting. Higher in reading your word. Lord, you are speaking to us. Victory is ours, but we have to be in a place to receive it. God, we thank you for your word today. Help us to go higher, in Jesus' Name!

JANUARY 12

1 Thessalonians 5:11

So encourage each other and build each other up, just as you are already doing.

DECREE FOR TODAY: We decree that we will not allow the devilish distractions to take our minds off of Christ! God is bigger than distractions!

Father, in Jesus' Name, thank you for keeping us safe. We won't be afraid for the terror by night nor for the arrow that flieth by day. You are our habitation. Thank you for the angels that keep watch over us daily. We appreciate Calvary. We appreciate your sufferings. Thank you for defeating the enemy of our souls; and even now, when the enemy comes in like a flood, the Spirit of the Lord will lift up a standard against him. In Jesus' Name, we thank you!

JANUARY 13

1 Timothy 6:6

But godliness with contentment is great gain.

DECREE FOR TODAY: We decree that we will respond with a soft answer; it turned away wrath!

Father, in Jesus' Name, thank you for joy. Your word declares that they that sow in tears shall reap in joy. Your kingdom, your presence within us, is not meat and drink, but righteousness and peace, and joy in the Holy Ghost. We will greatly rejoice in you, Lord, and our souls shall be joyful in the God of our salvation. You have clothed us with salvation. Glory to God! You have covered us with the robe of righteousness. Thank you for the word of God that is unto us joy and rejoicing of our hearts. In Jesus' Name, we thank you!

JANUARY 14

Mark 11:23

Truly I tell you, if anyone says to this mountain, 'Go, throw yourself into the sea,' and does not doubt in their heart but believes that what they say will happen, it will be done for them.

DECREE FOR TODAY: We decree that the blood of Jesus is still as fresh and powerful today as it was at Calvary!

Father, in Jesus' Name, thank you for the joy of the Lord which is our strength! Glory! We bless your Name today for being our strong tower. We can run into the Name of Jesus and be safe. You are the lifter of the bowed down head. The restorer of all that was lost. The keeper when we don't feel like being kept because of circumstances. Hallelujah! Thank you for renewing our minds, Lord. Satan desires to sift us as wheat but you have prayed for us! Oh God! Thank you for the Holy Ghost, the power that lives inside of us that allows us to go through, to walk on the devil's head, and to praise you even when the spirit of heaviness tries to overtake us. We will say Hallelujah! Hallelujah to our God! You are mighty in battle. Thank you for fighting for us. Thank you for being great inside of us, our Comforter. All of our battles are already won! Hallelujah! Thank you for victory, in Jesus' Name!

JANUARY 15

1 Corinthians 16:13

Be on your guard; stand firm in the faith; be courageous; be strong.

DECREE FOR TODAY: We decree that we will trust the Lord with all of our hearts and not lean to our own understanding! Especially today

Father, in Jesus' Name, we will offer the sacrifice of praise every day, giving thanks to your name. Thank you that our salvation is of grace and not of works. Grace makes us heirs according to the hope of life. Thank you that we have redemption through the Blood of Jesus! Hallelujah! We claim salvation for our children, our extended families and our enemies. It is not your will that any should perish. We thank you for it, in Jesus' Name!

JANUARY 16

Romans 10:17

Consequently, faith comes from hearing the message, and the message is heard through the word about Christ.

DECREE FOR TODAY: We decree that we will not give place to the devil in our walk, our talk, whatever! Tell the devil God has empowered us to do so!

Father, in Jesus' Name, thank you for your presence going with us! And as you promised Israel, you will give rest to us, your people, Lord. We will be still and wait for you, Lord. We will not fret over those who prosper and carry out evil devices. You promised to satisfy those that are weary. You are our Creator. You don't faint or grow weary. You promised to give power to the faint and those that have no might, you will increase their strength. It is by the power of your Spirit, Lord, that we will abound in hope. Keep us. Make the devil behave, Lord. In Jesus' Name, we thank you!

JANUARY 17

1 Thessalonians 4:14

For we believe that Jesus died and rose again, and so we believe that God will bring with Jesus those who have fallen asleep in him.

DECREE FOR TODAY: We decree that having done all, we will STAND!

Father, in Jesus' Name, thank you for guidance. Order our steps today and let us not go into the paths of the wicked. We rebuke the forces of hell that come against us. Your word promises us that you will guide us until we depart from this earth. Thank you! You will counsel us and afterward, receive us into glory. We await your glorious return, Lord. In the midst of uncertainties, you will make darkness light before us. Thank you Lord, in Jesus' Name.

JANUARY 18

Galatians 3:22

But Scripture has locked up everything under the control of sin, so that what was promised, being given through faith in Jesus Christ, might be given to those who believe.

DECREE FOR TODAY: We decree that we will esteem others better than ourselves!

Father, in Jesus' Name, thank you for being Lord, our God, the God of all flesh. There is nothing too hard for you. You are our refuge and strength, a very present help in the time of trouble. We are going to trust in you, Lord, with all of our hearts. We won't lean unto our own understanding on the job, in the home, or wherever! Keep our tongues today, Lord, so that we will have a soft answer for everyone, for it turneth away wrath. Help us to renew our minds, forgetting about the past and going forward in the spirit and power that you have given us! You are our Shepherd and we shall not want! You promised to supply every need according to your riches in glory by Christ Jesus. We yield our thoughts to you, Lord. We won't allow our thoughts to override your will. Let the Blood of Jesus cover us as we go out and come in, and we thank you for it, in Jesus' Name!

JANUARY 19

Ephesians 3:16-17

I pray that out of his glorious riches he may strengthen you with power through his Spirit in your inner being, so that Christ may dwell in your hearts through faith.

DECREE FOR TODAY: We decree that we will hold our peace!

Father, in Jesus' Name, thank you for the Name of Jesus. There is power in your Name. Healing in your Name! Deliverance in your Name! No other Name given whereby men can be saved! Your Name is a strong tower, Lord, and the righteous runneth into it and is safe! We're going to use the Name of JESUS today to pull down every strong hold. Every demon that steps into our territory today, we plead the blood of Jesus against it. Broken hearts today need mending, Lord. Help us to love everyone but to give our hearts to you, Lord. We thank you for the power that you give us to go through and not faint, in Jesus' Name!

JANUARY 20

Mark 11:24

Therefore I tell you, whatever you ask for in prayer, believe that you have received it, and it will be yours.

DECREE FOR TODAY: We decree that we will not grow weary, we will not faint! God is our strength and there is no failure in him. Tell the devil it is so!

Father, in Jesus' Name, thank you Lord God for victory in every area of our lives. Ah, Lord God, there is nothing too hard for you. You put the stars in place. You know them by name. How much more about your people. You reign, Lord. Thank you for making us peculiar people, royal priests, a holy nation, and chosen for your purpose. Glory to God! You knew us, Lord, before you formed us. What power! Thank you for the opportunity for you to dwell inside of us! Hallelujah! Thank you for the faith that is in us that moves the mountains in our lives. We claim victory over this day. We will not allow the forces of evil to control our atmosphere! Thank you God, in Jesus' Name!

JANUARY 21

Hebrews 11:1

Now faith is confidence in what we hope for and assurance about what we do not see.

DECREE FOR TODAY: ***We decree that no weapon formed against us regardless of its nature shall prosper! Tell the devil God said so!***

Father, in Jesus' Name, we stand in awe of your grace and mercy that continues to follow us day after day. Thank you, Lord! You amaze us with the simplicity of your Word and prayer that continue to strengthen us, encourage us and help us to endure this life. This precious gift of your Spirit that keeps us afloat, though we can't see it, we can feel the power and we can see the results of it. Who wouldn't serve a God like you, Lord! You make us laugh in the midst of chaos. You give us joy when the things around us seem to be crumbling. Lord Jesus, thank you for the precious gift of hope that you give us when things look hopeless! You amaze us, God. In Jesus' Name we thank you!

JANUARY 22

Romans 15:13

May the God of hope fill you with all joy and peace as you trust in him, so that you may overflow with hope by the power of the Holy Spirit.

DECREE FOR TODAY: ***We decree that the Word of God is our sword. We will hold our peace!***

Father, in Jesus' Name, we lift up those that are in the military today, protecting our country from harm. We ask that you will cover each soldier under the blood of Jesus. Let there be no lack in their lives, Lord. Let the angels cover them daily. Comfort them wherever they are, knowing that your watchful eyes see everything. You can handle whatever they encounter. You are our battle-axe. Bless their families, Lord. Cover their wives and children under the blood. Let your Spirit lift their spirits into a zone where they know without a doubt that you are with them. We praise you for answering, Lord, and in Jesus' Name, we thank you!

JANUARY 23

James 1:6
But when you ask, you must believe and not doubt, because the one who doubts is like a wave of the sea, blown and tossed by the wind.

DECREE FOR TODAY: We decree that we will not let our hearts be troubled!

Father, in Jesus' Name, we thank you for the Name of Jesus. There's power in your Name, Lord. The Name of the Lord is a strong tower and the righteous runneth into it and is safe. Lord help us to remember the power that is in your Name. We are going to say the Name of JESUS today. It has authority over every situation in our lives. You are the answer, Lord. You are our confidence! Our strong tower! Our deliverer! Our comforter when things seem to be overwhelming. God, we thank you! Bless the children today Lord. Keep them under your blood. Cover them in the schools today. The enemy desires to sift the children as wheat. We plead the blood of Jesus over them! Bless the teachers Lord. Cover them today. Thank you Lord, in Jesus' Name!

JANUARY 24

2 Corinthians 5:7
For we live by faith, not by sight.

DECREE FOR TODAY: We decree that God has equipped us to face every obstacle that the enemy presents!

Father, in Jesus' Name, thank you for the power of the Holy Ghost. It helps us to walk in your word. It is our Comforter when we need comforting. It is truth. It enables us to see clearly, so that we cannot be deceived. It helps us to be at peace with all men. It is the anointing within us that breaks every yoke. We pray for those that have not received your Spirit, that they will repent, acknowledge belief in your death, burial, and resurrection and accept you as Lord of their lives. Then, Lord, we pray that you will fill them with the gift of the Holy Ghost. Thank you for the outpouring, in Jesus' Name.

JANUARY 25

Hebrews 11:6
And without faith it is impossible to please God, because anyone who comes to him must believe that he exists and that he rewards those who earnestly seek him.

DECREE FOR TODAY: We decree that though it tarry, we will wait for it. It shall surely come!

Father, in Jesus' Name, thank you for being who you are. You never change! You are the same yesterday, today and you will be the same tomorrow! Glory! You are dependable, unstoppable, and unconquerable. You are well able to take down the plots of the enemy. Hallelujah! Today we will shake off everything that attacks the mind and the body like Paul shook off the viper and no harm came to him. We will shake off things, in the Name of Jesus! We refuse to be weighed down and heavy. You've given us a garment of praise for the spirit of heaviness. We praise you! We honor you! We adore you! We believe no weapon formed against us shall prosper! In Jesus' Name, we thank you!

JANUARY 26

1 Corinthians 12:26
If one member suffers, all suffer together; if one member is honored, all rejoice together.

DECREE FOR TODAY: We decree that we will pray, pray, and pray until God answers! We won't move! He is faithful!

Father, in Jesus' Name, thank you for healing of the minds, Lord. Make our feet like hinds feet so that we can mentally leap over our circumstances. Victory belongs to us. Peace belongs to us. Prosperity belongs to us. Pain-free bodies belong to us. We speak it into being. We are calling those things that are not as though they were! We are looking unto Jesus the author and finisher of our faith! We won't be shaken. We won't retreat. We won't allow our past to interfere with our thinking towards our future! Glory to God! In the midst of our storms, our rough times, and obstacles trying to hinder your people, we will stand anyhow. We won't be moved, Lord. We thank you for the strength you have supplied that enables us to go forward, in Jesus' Name!

JANUARY 27

<u>Psalm 29:11</u>
The Lord will give strength to His people; the Lord will bless his people with peace.

DECREE FOR TODAY: We decree that it is well with our soul! Nothing (but ourselves) can stop the plans that God has for us.

Father, in Jesus' Name, thank you for the promise that if we delight ourselves in you, you will give us the desires of our hearts, according to your will! You promised the desire of the righteous shall be granted. Glory to God! You said ask, and we shall receive! You are able to do exceedingly abundantly above all that we ask or think! And, Lord, we know that it is according to the power that works in us! Thank you for the power, Lord! We will take on Abraham's attitude. We will not stagger at your promise. We will be strong in faith, giving you all the glory! We are fully persuaded – we have been made to believe that what you have promised, you are well able to perform! We believe it, we claim it and we receive your promises to us, Lord! You will provide. You will heal! You will deliver! God, we thank you, in Jesus' Name!

JANUARY 28

<u>Ephesians 6:10</u>
I am strong in the Lord and in the power of His might.

DECREE FOR TODAY: We decree that the favor or God is upon us!

Father, in Jesus' Name, thank you that all of your commandments stand sure! Thank you, Lord, for being so gracious and full of compassion. You promised to remember the righteous. Lord, you said they shall not be afraid of evil tidings for their hearts are fixed, trusting in you! And, Lord, many today are like David was when he was going through, and he said his tears had been his meat day and night; and, people were asking him where is your

God? But, David asked his soul, why are thou disquieted and cast down? He encouraged himself and said he would yet praise you for your presence. Help us to encourage our souls; Lord, you promised that your presence will go with us. Dry the tears of your weeping people today, Lord, for you promised Joy will surely come. Thank you Lord, in Jesus' Name!

JANUARY 29

Ephesians 6:11
I have put on the complete armor of God.

DECREE FOR TODAY: We decree that our defense depends upon God!

Father, in Jesus' Name, we thank you for the opportunity to worship you and serve you in freedom without being persecuted, without being sawn asunder as the saints of old were. Oh, we appreciate this freedom. Glory to God! When you speak, there is peace and rest in our souls! You know our names, you know our addresses, and you know the number of hairs on our heads. You are the keeper of our souls, and on this day, we are going to trust in you and lean not to our own understanding. In situations during this day when we don't know what to do next, we will do nothing. We will wait on you, Lord, for the victory! In Jesus' Name, we thank you!

JANUARY 30

Isaiah 40:29
God gives power to the weak. And to those who have no might, He increases strength.

DECREE FOR TODAY: We decree that we are the children of Abraham by faith and all of the promises of God are yea and amen.

Father, in Jesus' Name, thank for your compassions. They fail not. Great is your Name, Lord! There's power in your Name. Thank you for giving us the authority to use your Name. It heals, it delivers, and it saves. Glory to God! Your presence in us makes us special! Chosen! Royal! Help us to realize and value the richness of your presence within us. We need not fret, fear, worry or become weary. Your strength enables us to do all things through Christ that strengthens us. Victory is ours! Peace is ours! We command it to be so in our lives. In Jesus' Name, we thank you Lord!

JANUARY 31

<u>Psalm 46:1</u>

God is my refuge and strength, a very present help in trouble.

DECREE FOR TODAY: We decree that we will not fear, even a confederacy! We will take on David's attitude: "I will not be afraid of tens of thousands of people who have set themselves against me on every side". Hide it in your heart!

Father, in Jesus' Name, thank you for creating VICTORY for us. Victory is our name. We decree it over every situation standing in front of us today. Your word declares that the angel of the Lord encampeth round about them that fear Him and deleverith them! Glory! You are in our midst, and whosoever hearkens to you shall dwell safely and shall be quiet from fear of evil! Thank you for knowing that when the enemy comes in like a flood, regardless of the enemy's form, we know that the Spirit of the Lord shall lift up a standard against him. We rebuke fear, poverty, discouragement, and sadness. Those spirits have to go, in Jesus' Name! Peace, joy and prosperity belong to your people. We speak it! In Jesus' Name, we thank you!

FEBRUARY 1

<u>Exodus 15:2</u>

The Lord is my strength and my song, And He is become my salvation.

DECREE FOR TODAY: We decree that we will make every effort to do everything without murmuring and disputing so that we can be blameless and harmless, the children of God, without rebuke in the midst of a chaotic world!

Father, in Jesus' Name, thank you for knowing our down-sittings and our uprisings. You understand our thoughts afar off. You are acquainted with all of our ways. You know every word in our tongues. How precious are your thoughts towards us. We can't number them Lord. They are more than sand! You are our strength! You are our salvation! We shall live and not die! Order our steps in your word, Lord. This day is the day that you have made. We will rejoice in it. We will not fear! We will not doubt! We will not go back! Looking unto you Lord from whence cometh our help, in Jesus' Name!

FEBRUARY 2

Deuteronomy 34:7

Like Moses, my eyesight shall not be dim nor shall my natural vigor be abated.

DECREE FOR TODAY: We decree that we will not fear the "unknown." God is already there!

Father, in Jesus' Name, thank you that when we woke up this morning everything was still in place. You didn't let the earth shake and move us about Lord God! We bless you. We will not forget your benefits for us. You are the healer of all diseases. Lord, you redeemed us from destruction. You are merciful and gracious. You have not dealt with us after our sins nor rewarded us according to our iniquities. You have removed our transgressions from us. Thank you, Lord God! You remembered that we are just dust. Help us to always keep in mind that you are round about your people. Your eyes are running to and fro beholding the good and the evil, and watching over us; for you never sleep. God we thank you, in Jesus' Name!

FEBRUARY 3

Joshua 1:9

God has commanded me. I am strong and very courageous in Christ; I am not afraid, nor dismayed, for the LORD my God is with me wherever I go.

DECREE FOR TODAY: We decree that we will not allow the cares of this world to trouble our spirits! Absolutely not! Shake it off!!!

Father, in Jesus' Name, you have blessed us to see another day this side of eternity. Thank you! We give you honor for who you are. You continue to allow daylight to appear so that we can go about our plans. You shut it down and give us night so that we can rest. Hallelujah! And, Lord, today we pray for our children around the world that are facing so many things – peer pressure, and things we never faced when growing up; and bullying, all kinds of demonic forces pulling after them. But, Lord, your blood still works and we plead the blood over our young people. Some parents are hurting as their children hurt, some are hurting because of disobedience, and some are hurting because, for whatever reason, distance separates them from families. But we know you are the same God wherever they are. You have loaned the children to the parents to raise them to serve you, and God help us to carry out the task as parents so that they will give you glory. We thank you for life, Lord. Bless us throughout this day to be a blessing to someone else. In Jesus' Name, we thank you!

FEBRUARY 4

1 Samuel 2:10

Christ has made me a king and priest to God. God will give strength to his king and exalt the horn of his anointed.

DECREE FOR TODAY: We decree that we will not be carried away with every wind of doctrine. We will walk in truth!

Father, in Jesus' Name, thank you for all you've done; in the past! Lord, you opened doors, made ways out of no way and brought down high places. Glory to God. Thank you! And, Lord, we pray for the elderly. Many have been forsaken by their children. Many don't even have families to bring them a glass of water when wanted, but are having to wait on someone else to do it. Lord Jesus! You told us to bear one another's burdens. We pray today, Lord God, that it will be a good day for the elderly that have been through so much. Waiting, waiting and waiting. Lord, we pray for those dead beat children that have forsaken their parents, forgotten about them, and left them in nursing homes to fend for themselves; some are in helpless situations. Some children have forgotten that their parents went through many trials to raise them. Wake them up, Lord God. Thank you for doing it, in Jesus' Name!

FEBRUARY 5

1 Samuel 30:6

I strengthen myself in the LORD my God.

DECREE FOR TODAY: We decree that God has equipped us to face every obstacle that the enemy places in front us and come through victoriously! God said so!

Father, in Jesus' Name, thank you for making us victorious. Thank you for giving us the ability to stand. Having done all, we will stand, Lord. We thank you for making us more than conquerors trough Christ Jesus. Thank you for the blood of Jesus that has washed away our sins. Thank you for wiping the slate clean. Thank you that you don't bring up our past and you give us the power to forget about it. Your grace is unmeasurable. Your love is unexplainable. We appreciate you, Lord. Great is thy faithfulness unto us. In Jesus' Name, we thank you!

FEBRUARY 6

2 Samuel 22:40

God has armed me with strength for battle; He has subdued under me those who rose against me.

DECREE FOR TODAY: We decree that this joy that we have, the world didn't give it to us and the world can't take it away! Tell the devil it is so!!

Father, in Jesus' Name, thank you for lifting our eyelids this morning. And, Lord, I heard you say worship. So, we take this time to worship you and not spend it asking for things. But, we give you glory for who you are. We magnify you for your greatness, for taking the dust of the earth and breathing into us the breath of life. Thank you, Lord God! Hallelujah! We praise you for salvation. We don't thank you enough for pulling us out of the fire and giving us power over the devil and the demons of hell. Thank you, Lord God! Help us to make this day be a day of worship, and a day of dedication to you in praise. Help us not to ask you for anything this day but to thank you for what you have already done! Glory to God! In Jesus' Name!

FEBRUARY 7

Nehemiah 8:10

The joy of the Lord is my strength.

DECREE FOR TODAY: We decree that we will hold our peace in the home, on the job, or wherever! Moving without God's directions will result in disaster!

Father, in Jesus' Name, thank you for your word that comforts us on every side. Thank you for the armour that helps us to be able to stand against the wiles of the devil. Thank you that we are not ignorant of Satan's devices, so he can't take advantage of us. Bless your Name, Lord! Thank you for keeping the seas within their borders so that they didn't overflow and drown us during the night! God, we thank you! Your Word tells us to be courageous, to stand in the faith and to be strong! Knowing, Lord God, that our light affliction is but for a moment! Hallelujah! In Jesus' Name, we thank you!

FEBRUARY 8

<u>Psalm 18:1</u>
I will love You, O Lord, my Strength.

DECREE FOR TODAY: We decree that we will take on the "so what" attitude! God is in control of our lives as we yield to him! No weapon formed against us shall prosper. Tell the devil, God said so!

Father, in Jesus' Name, it is a day of thanksgiving. Thanking you for the gift of praise. It lifts heaviness. It takes us to a place of glory! Hallelujah! Thank you, Lord, for making ways out of no way, opening closed doors, healing our bodies, renewing our minds, restoring things that were broken. Thanking you in advance for those things that are yet to be put in place, for bringing down our high places, lifting us from the valleys. You are the thread that holds families together and brings peace in the midst of confusion. God, we give you glory! Thank you for going into areas unnoticed when we need you most and showing yourself strong on our behalf! You are our Rock! Thank you, Lord, that you have made us winners in advance. We will not fear nor be dismayed for our God is in control. In Jesus' Name, we thank you Lord!

FEBRUARY 9

<u>Psalm 28:7-8</u>
The LORD is my strength and my shield, and my saving refuge.

DECREE FOR TODAY: We decree that we will trust the Lord with all of our hearts and not lean to our own understanding! Especially today!

Father, in the Name of Jesus, today is a day of acknowledgement of your greatness in the earth. Thank you, God, for your love and for creating us from the dust of the earth and allowing us to sit in heavenly places. Lord God, you are awesome! Thank you for mercy. Though we have short-comings, you look beyond our faults and see our needs. Thank you for blessing us with children! Thank you for family! Oh how excellent is your Name in all the earth. God, we thank you for allowing us to read your word. Oh how amazing it is that just reading your word lifts our spirits, gives us hope and renews our minds! Thank you for the mind to be able to sift the positive from the negative. We give you glory, Lord, for giving us victory in every situation, in Jesus' Name!

FEBRUARY 10

Psalm 29:11
The LORD will give strength to his people.

DECREE FOR TODAY: We decree that we will not give place to the devil in our walk, our talk, or whatever! Tell the devil, God has empowered us to do so!

Father, in Jesus' Name, we bless you, Lord! We thank you for granting your riches in glory to your people. Thank you for strengthening us and energizing us with your power through the Holy Ghost. Thank you for the faith that dwells in our hearts through you, Lord. Thank you for keeping us rooted and grounded in your love! Your endless love is beyond understanding, and we are grateful to you. We surrender ourselves to you so that you can flood our lives with your presence. Thank you for doing more than we can ask or think according to your power that works in us. We are going to imitate you and walk in the love toward others, as you love us. We will value each other and have compassion for one another without partiality. Use us in your kingdom and help us to walk wisely, making the most of our time on earth and giving all the glory to you, Lord. In Jesus' Name, we thank you!

FEBRUARY 11

Psalm 59:9
God is my defense.

DECREE FOR TODAY: We decree that having done all, we will STAND!

Father, in Jesus' Name, we come before your throne; from the ends of the earth, your people are crying out to you. Some hearts are overwhelmed, Lord. But, we know you will lead all of your people to the Rock that is higher than us! You have been our shelter. You have been our strong tower and you have sheltered us from the enemy! We will dwell in your presence. You have heard our vows. We reverence you, Lord. You have given an inheritance to those that fear you. We adore your Name. We will use it in the earth, for there is POWER in your Name! You have appointed mercy and truth to watch over us. We say thank you, Lord! We will trust confidently in you day after day. You are our rock of unyielding strength. You are our refuge. Power belongs to you! In Jesus' Name, we thank you Lord!

FEBRUARY 12

Psalm 68:35

The God of Israel is He who gives strength and power to His people.

DECREE FOR TODAY: We decree that we will hold our peace!

Father, in Jesus' Name, we humbly approach your throne in boldness as you have given us the authority to come before you. Our souls long for you, Lord. We love your presence in our lives. We appreciate your love for the just and the unjust. All souls belong to you. Thank you for not casting us away in the midst of our sins. Your grace is unexplainable. Your divine care for your people can never be measured by human efforts. Oh how excellent is your name in all the earth. You are our source, our defense, and our help in the times of difficult moments. You are the strength of our lives. Thank you for the hope that lies within us. We pray for the bereaved families today, Lord. So much sorrow in the land but in spite of that, you still remain faithful. Thank you for peace in the mind, in the home, and on the job. Thank you that you have given us power over the atmosphere and angels to protect it. We give you glory Lord in Jesus' Name!

FEBRUARY 13

Psalm 73:26

God is the strength of my heart and my portion forever.

DECREE FOR TODAY: God is our rock and our salvation. He is the rock of our strength!

Father, in Jesus' Name, thank you for blessing and giving favor to your people that walk in your ways, keep your word and continually seek your face. We pray that we will not wander from your commandments through ignorance or willful disobedience. Open our eyes, Lord, to spiritual truth so that we can continue to understand your word and apply it to our daily lives. Remove from us the way of falsehood and unfaithfulness. Help us to continue to trust in you as our ROCK! You are our portion! Give us teachable hearts! We hope and wait with complete confidence in you, Lord. In Jesus' Name, we thank you Lord!

FEBRUARY 14

Proverbs 24:5

A wise man is strong. Yes, a man of knowledge increases strength. God gives abundant wisdom to me without finding fault.

DECREE FOR TODAY: We decree that we will allow the glory of Lord to rise among us! Ignore distractions and demonic activity taking place around us, for God has given us the victory!

Father, in Jesus' Name, we thank you for hearing our prayers. Our supplications are before you, Lord. We thank you for your faithfulness and not judging us according to the sins we have committed. All of us have been persecuted by the enemy. Some feel as though they have been crushed to the ground and are in a dark place. Some feel overwhelmed in the spirit and their hearts are troubled today, Lord. Lift them up. You are the lifter of the bowed down heard. Help us to be pleasing in your sight. You are our God. We will be led by your Spirit. We pray for our enemies, all of those that try to afflict our lives. Let mercy prevail for them. We shout the victory! We shout Hallelujah! For you reign. We thank you for it in Jesus' Name!

FEBRUARY 15

Isaiah 28:6

The Lord gives strength to those who turn the battle at the gate.

DECREE FOR TODAY: We decree that God's favor is upon us! Nothing can stand against us successfully! No weapon! No weapon formed against us shall prosper.

Father, in Jesus' Name, thank you for being our Shepherd! Thank you for feeding us, guiding us and shielding us. Thank you for keeping our hearts in a quiet place. We give you glory for refreshing us and giving us life. And, Lord, we know that when we sleep, our heartbeat drops to its lowest level. When you wake us up, you raise it to the level where it should be. Thank you for not allowing the lowest heartbeat to just stop while we slept, else we would have gone into eternity overnight. You are good, Lord. Oh how marvelous you are! Thank you for your goodness and mercy that follow us day after day! Thank you for allowing us to dwell in your presence all of our days! We give you glory and thanks, in Jesus' Name!

FEBRUARY 16

Luke 18:27
The things which are impossible with men are possible with God.

DECREE FOR TODAY: We decree that we will tell God THANK YOU! Thank you for the good times! Thank you for the trials and tribulations. Thank you! Thank you! Thank you Lord!

Father, in Jesus' Name, it is a day of thanksgiving! We give you glory for all, things because everything is working for our good! Hallelujah! Thank you for every mountain, because we know they must come down. Thank you for every trial, for you told us to count it all joy! We praise you for every battle, because they belong to you and not us! Glory to God! We honor you for meeting every need! Thank you, Jesus. And, Lord, for those that are weeping, we thank you for the joy that will come in the morning. Most of all, we thank you for this great plan of salvation. Thank you for delivering us from the powers of darkness. Thank you for families, Lord. Oh, how wonderful your divine plan is, that includes families. Thank you, because it is in you that we live and move and have our being! In Jesus' Name, we give you glory!

FEBRUARY 17

Romans 15:5
May God, who gives this patience and encouragement, help you live in complete harmony with each other, as is fitting for followers of

Christ Jesus.

DECREE FOR TODAY: We decree that we will be happy and not walk in the council of the ungodly!

Father, in Jesus' Name, thank you for your anointing that refreshes us day after day. We give you glory for who you are, Lord! There is none like you. Your love for us is beyond expression. Thank you for grace! Thank you for your patience in the earth. Thank you for not wiping us out because of the turmoil that is going on in the earth. Thank you for your presence in the atmosphere. Thank you for dispatching angels to watch over us. Hallelujah! We adore you, Lord! You are precious to us. You refresh us. You keep our minds intact. You cause our memories to continue to flow! Glory to God! You've not rewarded us for our sins. Thank you for forgiveness. Bless the children, Lord. Keep them from violence. Keep them covered under the blood. Fill them with the gift of the Holy Ghost. Help us to be ready for your return, Lord. In Jesus' Name, we thank you!

FEBRUARY 18

Proverbs 12:25

Anxiety in a man's heart weighs it down, but an encouraging word makes it glad.

DECREE FOR TODAY: We decree that the blessing of the Lord it maketh rich and he addeth no sorrow with it! Tell the devil, God said so!

Father, in Jesus' Name, thank you for your presence in the earth, daily controlling everything that involves your people. Thank you for peace, love and joy in our hearts. And, Lord, many are going through rough places but you promised that we would go through the waters and you will be with us, through the rivers and you won't let them overwhelm us, nor will you allow the fire to burn us. Thank you that our trials make us stronger, make us trust you more, Lord, and cause us to see your miraculous works in our lives. Glory to God! We have put on the whole armor and having done all we will STAND! Joy is ours! Peace is ours! Victory is guaranteed! We will declare your Name in the earth! We praise you for the power of the Holy Ghost that puts us in control of our minds, our surroundings, our encounters and guarantees us victory. We are more than conquerors through you, Lord. Help us to daily operate under your anointing, for it will break every yoke! We will stand. We won't take down! We won't go back! We will fight this good fight of faith through you, Lord, in Jesus' Name!

FEBRUARY 19

Isaiah 49: 13
Sing for joy, O heavens! Rejoice, O earth! Burst into song, O mountains! For the LORD has comforted his people and will have compassion on them in their suffering.

DECREE FOR TODAY: We decree that we won't let anything or any person disturb our peace this day! We declare it to be so!

Father, in Jesus' Name, your mercy is prevailing. Your longsuffering is prevailing. Your kindness is prevailing. We are looking unto you Lord from whence cometh our help. The world is in need of you, Lord. We thank you for covering your people and hiding us in the secret place. Thank you for the confidence you have instilled in your people that are trusting you! We say Hallelujah! We say Glory! Our God reigns. Thank you God that you have not allowed the cares of this world to weigh us down. You said lay aside every weight, regardless of its nature! Thank you for keeping us in peace, in a restful place. We pray for those that are feeling discouraged, Lord. We ask that you will bless them. You are our hope. And, Lord, you said if we have hope in this world only, we are men most miserable. Thank you, Lord, that we can walk in victory and power, overcoming every obstacle because of the God in us! We take authority over the atmosphere around us. We rebuke the powers of darkness assigned to our cities. We take courage in knowing that you are our refuge, our strong tower, and nothing happens to us unless you allow it. Thank you, Lord, in Jesus' Name!

FEBRUARY 20

Colossians 3:2
Set your mind on things above, not on things on the earth.

DECREE FOR TODAY: We decree that we will not fear, even a confederacy!

Father, in Jesus' Name, thank you for this great gospel that saves, heals and delivers! We praise you, Lord! You know how to encourage, you know how to bless, and you know how to lift us above the spirits of the gods of this world. Glory to God! Thank you, Jesus, that we can use our minds to leap over negativity. We give you glory! Thank you for the secret place. Thank you for the prayer space in our hearts where we touch you and hear from you, Lord! What a miracle! You speak good things to us. You put us in the glory cloud. Your anointing causes us to soar in the spirit. It brings joy! It brings peace! It delivers! It breaks every yoke! It separates our own thoughts and causes yours to surface in our spirit. Glory to God! Happy is the man that makes you his God! Thank you for choosing your people to be possessed with your presence daily! Thank you that we can rest in you, for giving us favor, and for the Word of God that has all answers. In Jesus' Name, we praise you!

FEBRUARY 21

Colossians 3:23

Whatever you do, do it heartily, as to the Lord and not to men.

DECREE FOR TODAY: We decree that we are the children of Abraham by faith and all of the promises of God are yea and amen!

Father, in Jesus' Name, thank you that we can step out in faith, knowing that when we acknowledge you, you will direct our paths! We give you glory for this journey of faith! Bless your people today, Lord. We thank you for the oxygen that you so freely give us. Thank you for keeping our minds and giving us the ability to think right. What a privilege. Thank you for putting all of our faculties in place. What a Master Mind you are, Lord. We praise you for every high place that must come down, according to your word. Thank you for going out before us, protecting us, and warning us of what is ahead. Hallelujah! Thank you for the Joy that you give us in the midst of a chaotic world. Thank you for sweet sleep! Thank you for the angels that keep watch over us day after day! You are our ROCK! Our hiding place! Our secret dwelling place! Glory to God! Thank you for allowing us to be persecuted but not abandoned and struck down but not destroyed! Thank you, Lord, in Jesus' Name!

FEBRUARY 22

Proverbs 14:30

A peaceful heart leads to a healthy body; jealousy is like cancer in the bones.

DECREE FOR TODAY: We decree that the favor or God is upon us!

Father, in Jesus' Name, we bless you today for choosing us to be a part of your kingdom. We feel honored that the God that created the world has given us an opportunity to spend eternity with you, Lord! We are grateful! Thank you for every moment that you allow us to breathe in this universe. Where would we be without you, Lord? Thank you for every mountain you have brought us over. Thank you for every trial and every valley, for we get to know you better in the struggles of this life. You mount your people up, Lord! Thank you for prayer. Thank you for knowing that you hear us. Thank you for loving us beyond measure. Thank you for forgiveness. We've all come short of your glory, but you continue to have compassions every morning. Glory to God! Bless families, Lord. Mend brokenness. Heal sick bodies. Deliverer those bound by the powers of darkness. Wherever we are lacking in our walk with you, help us to step-up in prayer, in fasting, in reading your word, in dedication and whatever is needed to enable us to continue to leap for joy, to walk by faith, and to totally depend upon you. Thank you, Lord, in Jesus' Name!

FEBRUARY 23

Proverbs 3: 7-8

Don't be impressed with your own wisdom. Instead, fear the Lord and turn away from evil. Then you will have healing for your body and strength for your bones.

DECREE: We decree that we will pray, pray, and pray until God answers! We won't move! He is faithful!

Father, in Jesus' Name, thank you for opening our eyes to see another day! Oh how gracious you are, Lord! We won't take your goodness for granted! We lay ourselves before you in humble adoration and ask you for forgiveness of all of our sins. We repent of those wrong things that we have done purposely and unintentional. Oh, how gracious you are, Lord. Thank you for spreading the sky so that the sun and moon cover the entire earth. Oh, you have blessed us to move about in your Spirit that powerfully enables us to see spiritually and to grow in the knowledge of our Lord. Thank you for covering those on the battlefields, Lord. We thank you for this great freedom that we are enjoying. Thank you, God! Hallelujah! We pray for those that are being held captive in their minds by the powers of darkness. We pray for healing both spiritually and naturally. We pray for deliverance from strongholds in areas where the powers of darkness are ruling. We cast down every imagination that is not like you! Victory is ours! Peace is ours! Joy is ours! Thank you Lord, in Jesus' Name!

FEBRUARY 24

Psalms 63:5
You satisfy me more than the richest of foods.

DECREE FOR TODAY: We decree that we be still and let God take control! The battle is not ours

Father, in Jesus' Name, thank you! Hallelujah! Thank you! Thank you! Lord, we bless you for your faithfulness. There is much evil that has arisen in the world, Lord, but the sun is still rising in the earth. The Son is still rising in the lives your people that is powerful enough to overcome every evil force. Glory to God! Many have been hunted down and persecuted, but you did not desert anyone. Some have been cast down, but not destroyed! Still standing! Still proclaiming the Name of Jesus! There's power in your Name and we thank you for it. We are using your word to navigate through this world. You are our guide. You know the way! We will acknowledge you in all of our ways, knowing that you will direct our paths. Thank you for truth that will stand every test! We are moving forward even in our minds, Lord, pulling down every stronghold that exalts itself against the knowledge of God. Thank you, Lord God, in Jesus' Name!

FEBRUARY 25

Proverbs 3:7-8
Don't be impressed with your all wisdom. Instead, fear the Lord and turn your back on evil. Then you'll gain renewed health and vitality.

DECREE FOR TODAY: We decree that though it tarry, we will wait for it. It shall surely come!

Father, in Jesus' Name, we bless you for giving us this great day! Thank you for another chance to give you glory, and to experience the power of your love! What love! There is no greater love than yours, Lord! We delight ourselves in you. We are hiding your Word in our hearts so that we won't sin against you. We will not forget your Word. We will live by it and observe it. Thank you that we can see your Word in every situation that it speaks to. We lean on you, Lord. We trust in you! We are confident in you. The enemy cannot shake us from your presence. Thank you for the power! Thank you for the anointing that breaks every yoke. Thank you for teaching us how to use our minds as sifters to sift out everything that exalts itself against our thinking! Glory to God! Thank you for the Blood covering! It heals! It delivers! It wards off satanic influences! It broke the bands of bondage that were holding your people in darkness. There is so much power in your Blood, and we thank you for it, in Jesus' Name!

FEBRUARY 26

Isaiah 55: 1-2

Is anyone thirsty? Come and drink-even if you have no money! Take your choice of wine or milk-it's all free! Why spend your money on food that does not give you strength? Why pay for food that does you no good? Listen and I will tell you where to get food that is good for the soul!

DECREE FOR TODAY: We decree that God has equipped us to face every obstacle that the enemy places in front us and come through victoriously! God said so!

Father, in Jesus' Name, thank you for being our mighty God, our strong tower, our go-to in the time of need. Glory to God! Thank you for your presence right now in the earth. We praise you for arming us for this journey. Thank you for fighting our battles. All you require of us is to get out of your way and let go and let God! We thank you that you have taught us to fight spiritually and leave the natural battles to you to handle. Thank you for the strength to fight with the Word of God. We speak to every pain, every disappointment, every trial, every hard-place, and every thought that is not like you, and every disturbing moment and command those things to be released from the minds of your people, in Jesus' Name! We fight with faith against doubt! We exercise the authority that you have given to us to declare peace in families. We command the demonic forces of hell to get out of our surroundings and out of the atmosphere! Greater is he that is in us than he that is in the world! Thank you for the power of the Holy Ghost. Hallelujah! In Jesus' Name, we thank you Lord!

FEBRUARY 27

<u>Proverbs 3:5</u>

Trust in the Lord with all of your heart, and lean not unto your own understanding.

DECREE FOR TODAY: We decree that the Word of God is our sword. We will hold our peace!

Father, in Jesus' we honor your presence in us. We honor your presence in the earth. We thank you for this great privilege to know you, talk to you, to touch heaven, and to have access to the greatest authority that exits. Glory to God! Thank you, Jesus! Thank you for the blood that you shed. Hallelujah! It covers! Your stripes have provided healing! Your mercy and grace have kept us through unseen dangers. Your love has washed away all of our sins, all of our shortcomings, and all that is not like you! Yes, God, we thank you! Thank you for the ability to whisper a prayer to you in the midst of chaos! Thank you for answering! We lift your Name on high! Thank you for taking away pain! Thank you for protecting the children in that bullying environment! Thank you for being a friend. Thank you for being our help and loving us. We trust in you and you alone, Lord! In Jesus' Name, we praise you!

FEBRUARY 28

<u>Exodus 23:25</u>

You must serve only the Lord your God. If you do, I will bless you with food and water, and I will protect you from illness.

DECREE FOR TODAY: We decree that we will take heed that the liberty of ours does not become a stumbling block to them that are weak.

Father, in Jesus' Name, thank you being so awesome in our lives! Thank you, God, for the ability to have access to you. What a privilege! Thank you for favor. Thank you for choosing us and giving us an opportunity to experience the power you have put within us. Power that saves us. Power that heals us. Power that keeps us. Glory to God! Lord, we pray for everyone that is in a battle that seems to be getting the best of them. You declared that the battle belongs to you! Thank you for allowing us to cast our cares upon you for you care for us. Thank you for taking care of tomorrow. You have already been there. Thank you for the rest and peace you have given to your people. We bless you, Lord. We thank you that we can walk in victory, leaping over everything in our minds that tries to disturb us. Hallelujah, for the grace that you have so freely given to us! Thank you for the authority that is in your name! In Jesus' Name, we give you all the glory!

FEBRUARY 29

<u>Isaiah 58:11</u>

The Lord will guide you continually, watering your life when you are dry and keeping you healthy, too. You will be like a well-watered garden like an ever-flowing spring.

DECREE FOR TODAY: We decree that we will not grow weary, we will not faint! God is our strength and there is no failure in him. Tell the devil it is so!

Father, in the Name of Jesus, thank you for the Word of God that has been written for our learning, our inspiration, and our hope! Glory to God! Oh how great and powerful the Word of God is in our lives! It is our sword and, God, we thank you! We will use it to declare victory, declare healing, and declare deliverance in every area of our lives. Lord, you warned us that in the last days perilous times shall come, but you are still greater in us than he that is in the world! Thank you for your promise that blessed is the habitation of the just. Let our eyelids look straight before you, Lord, that we turn not to the right nor to the left. Help us to pray your word, Lord, for in it is life! Thank you Lord, in Jesus' Name!

MARCH 1

A cheerful heart does good like medicine, but a broken spirit makes one sick. Proverbs 17:22

DECREE FOR TODY: We decree that we will respond with a soft answer; it turned away wrath!

Father, in Jesus' Name, we give you glory! We praise you for your greatness, your excellency, your power, and your authority! Hallelujah! Thank you for keeping your people, enabling us to abound in the work of the Lord and keeping us planted on the solid Rock! Thank you for the gift of prayer, a simple way for us to reach you, Lord, a simple way for us to have every obstacle removed, bodies healed, deliverances, and whatever we need. You said ask and it shall be given according to your divine will! Thank you, Lord, for allowing us to be planted in you and giving us power over demonic forces so that they cannot uproot us! Glory to God! We bless you, Lord, for the air you provide for us to breathe freely. Thank you for the victory in all things, in Jesus' Name!

MARCH 2

Psalms 119: 93

I will never forget your commandments, for you have used them to restore my joy and health.

DECREE FOR TODY: We decree that we will respond with a soft answer; it turns away wrath!

Father, in Jesus' Name, we give you glory and honor for a brand new day! A day of joy! A day of thanksgiving! A day of repentance! A day to do some good for somebody else regardless of our state, even if it is just speaking a kind word! Thank you for your lovingkindness that has blessed your people with life itself. What an opportunity to go through this world with the Blessed Hope of life eternal. Glory to God! Thank you, Jesus. And while we tabernacle in this flesh, we will obey your word. It has a promise that your blessings will overtake us. Thank you for the strength you supply us with that takes us from strength to strength. Glory to God! Bless the children today, Lord. Cover them. We rebuke the spirit of bullying that is affecting so many children. We bind the hands of the enemy. Cover them, Lord. We thank you for it, in Jesus' Name!

MARCH 3

Psalms 145:15-16

The eyes of all look to you in hope; you give them their food as they need it. When you open your hand, you satisfy the hunger and thirst of every living thing.

DECREE FOR TODY: We decree that this is God's day! He made it for us, and we will rejoice in it and be glad!

Father, in the Name of Jesus, thank you for redeeming us by the precious blood of Jesus! Glory to God! Thank you for choosing us, making your people, a special people, and chosen before the foundation of the world! Thank you for inspiring your prophets and apostles to write the word of God. Oh, it is precious to us, Lord! Your Word changes lives and works miracles! Oh Lord, the Word of God is so powerful! It is our sword! It is our defense! We can speak your Word and watch it work by faith – it moves mountains, brings down high places – time and time again it has healed us! Glory to God. We thank you for your presence in the earth that keeps the powers of darkness under control, Hallelujah! In Jesus' Name, we thank you!

MARCH 4

Exod.23:25

You shall serve the Lord your God; He shall bless your bread and water, and I will take sickness from your midst.

DECREE FOR TODAY: We decree that we will shake ourselves from the cares of this world and remind ourselves that Jesus said, in the world we will have much tribulation but we will be of good cheer because Jesus has overcome the world!

Father, in Jesus' Name, we thank you for all things! So many times, Lord, we approach you asking, but we come to you with a heart of thanksgiving! Thank you for waking us! You could have allowed us to sleep into eternity, but you spared us and have given us another opportunity to worship you, to give you glory, to make things right, and to set our houses in order. Glory to God! Thank you, Lord, that you have not shut down the rain. You continue to supply us with water from heaven, something man can't do. You continue to arm us spiritually for the spiritual battles that are set before us that are not ours, but yours. You arm our souls and our bodies to mentally stand against the wiles of the devil. You empower us with spiritual boldness to face every trial, every test, and to overcome every obstacle. And, Lord, we thank you for Faith that can conquer anything! Thank you for the Blood of Jesus that has rescued us from the power of sin! In Jesus' Name, we thank you Lord!

MARCH 5

<u>2 Corinthians 12:10</u>

For the sake of Christ, then, I am content with weaknesses, insults, hardships, persecutions, and calamities. For when I am weak, then I am strong.

DECREE FOR TODAY: We decree that we will NOT render evil for evil! The battle is not ours. It belongs to the Lord!

Father, in Jesus' Name, thank you for a fresh anointing! We give you glory for your presence in the earth! Without you, Lord, we would be hopeless in this corrupt world. But thanks be to God who gives us the victory through our Lord Jesus Christ! Thank you God! Thank you for your strategic plans towards mankind. Thank you, Lord, for loving us and miraculously creating for us a brain that supernaturally talks to the rest of the body and causes our fingers to move, and our hands to move! It talks to our minds so that when we are ready to stand up, the brain has communicated! Hallelujah, Jesus! Glory to God! We praise you, Lord! How mighty you are, Lord! We are grateful for this great plan of salvation – your grace and mercy spared us. Your compassions fail not! You have cast our sins into the sea of forgetfulness! Bless your people today to be a blessing to someone else. We thank you for it, in Jesus' Name!

MARCH 6

<u>Philippians 4:13</u>

I can do all things through him who strengthens me.

DECREE FOR TODAY: We decree that we will not allow the noise of the world to disturb us! God has overcome the world!

Father, in Jesus' Name, we lift up our eyes unto the hills from whence cometh our help! Our help comes from the Lord, the God that never sleeps nor slumbers. Hallelujah! You are our keeper and our shade! Thank you for preserving our going out and our coming in. They that trust in you shall be as Mt. Zion which cannot be moved but abideth forever! You have done great things for us, Lord. Those that are sowing in tears shall reap in joy! The bowed down head shall be lifted! The needs of the needy shall be provided! The sick will be healed. The broken will be mended! Glory to God! We speak life, for the power of life and death is in the tongue. Blessed is everyone that walks in your ways. They shall eat the good of the land! Thank you Lord, in Jesus' Name!

MARCH 7

Philippians 4:19

And my God will supply every need of yours according to his riches in glory in Christ Jesus.

DECREE FOR TODAY: We decree that God sees our lives as finished products! We need only let God take us through the earthly process! Nothing can stop Him!

Father, in Jesus' Name, we thank you for this day! We praise you for being in the land of the living. We don't take it lightly, Lord. Glory to your Name. We thank you for those that sacrificed their lives in the Military to protect us, Lord! We thank you for those that are still serving to keep us safe. Bless them. Cover them with your blood. Bless their families. We thank you for the families' sacrifices. We are grateful. We ask that you will comfort the families of those that are away from their loved ones and that are serving and those that have suffered loss. You are our strength, our strong tower, our healer and deliverer. Mighty is your hand in the earth, Lord! We pray for those that don't know you as Savior. We pray that they will seek you as we approach these end times, Lord. We pray for the young people, those that are participating in the violent acts across this nation. We bind the hands of the enemy that is using them. Rescue their minds! We thank you for it, in Jesus' Name!

MARCH 8

Matthew 6:26

Look at the birds of the air: they neither sow nor reap nor gather into barns, and yet your heavenly Father feeds them. Are you not of more value than they?

DECREE FOR TODAY: We decree that we will not allow the enemy to occupy any space in our atmosphere today! When we see him coming, in our spirit we will plead the blood of Jesus against him! It's our space in God! He has no right to enter!

Father, in Jesus' Name, thank you for your continued guidance. Thank you for your greatness; you are the Great I AM; you are the one who formed the mountains and created the winds. You keep the rivers and oceans full so that we have water to drink day after day. Glory to God! You are awesome, Lord. There is none like you in heaven and earth! You keep covenant and showing mercy and loving kindness to your people who walk before you with all their hearts. We will wait and hope for and expect you to move in our situations. We will be brave and of good courage. We won't let our hearts be troubled but rather enduring! We hope in your word, Lord, for you are our Rock and the firm strength of our hearts. You are our shield and the lifter of our heads! Thank you, God, in Jesus' Name!

MARCH 9

Matthew 6:28

And why are you anxious about clothing? Consider the lilies of the field, how they grow: they neither toil nor spin.

DECREE FOR TODAY: We decree that we will not fear man for God shall bring every hidden thing to light!

Father, in Jesus' Name, we give you glory for the peace and harmony from you that rules in our hearts and that settle the questions that arise in our minds! You have called us to that peace! We are appreciative and thankful for your love! Thank you for the Word that declares your people will dwell in a peaceable habitation, in safe dwellings and quiet resting places both spiritually and naturally. We declare it to be so in our personal lives, Lord. Your word declares that the effect of righteousness will be peace both internal and external and the end result of it will be quietness and confident trust in you forever! Glory to God! Before you formed us, you knew us and picked us out to be chosen vessels, royal priesthood, and special for your glory! Thank you for your strength that takes from strength to strength, in Jesus' Name!

MARCH 10

Matthew 6:34

Therefore do not be anxious about tomorrow, for tomorrow will be anxious for itself. Sufficient for the day is its own trouble.

DECREE FOR TODAY: We decree that we are convinced and sure of this very thing that the Lord, He who has begun a good work in us will complete it until the day of Jesus Christ!

Father, in Jesus' Name, thank you for hope, thank you for life, and thank you for your divine intervention in the affairs of man. Thank you for watching our comings and our goings! We praise you for empowering us and directing our paths and not allowing us to stray into the paths of wickedness. Your glory is revealed in the earth. We praise you for divine protection and division. When the enemy comes in like a flood, the Spirit of the Lord will lift up a standard against him! Glory to God! Thank you for deliverance from the powers of darkness; thank you for delivering our tongues, our speech, our thinking and sealing our minds so that we can sift everything that is not like you! Glory to God! We praise you for the food, the water, the cold, the hot, the sunshine, the moon and all of these things that we take for granted! You are awesome, Lord. In Jesus' Name, we thank you!

MARCH 11

Romans 5:2

Through him we have also obtained access by faith into this grace in which we stand, and we rejoice in hope of the glory of God.

DECREE FOR TODAY: We decree that we will not be intimidated by the whispers of demonic forces. Greater is he that is in us than he that is in the world! God said so!

Father, in Jesus' Name, we praise you, Lord! We give you glory! Oh, how excellent is your Name in all the earth! Your Name is above all Names! Your strength goes beyond that of humans. Your forgiveness is matchless. Your longsuffering and patience is far beyond that of your creation and yet you have made your Spirit available to us so that we can pattern our lives after you! Glory to God! We can see that it is evening time! Thank you for providing us with the Word of God that empowers us to speak our way through these days of uncertainty in the earth. You are the God of the earth. You are in control of everything that exists. Thank you for the assurance, Lord, that we can have joy and peace in a corrupt environment. Oh, how marvelous you are! The gift of Faith is our passport. Thank you Lord, in Jesus' Name!

MARCH 12

2 Corinthians 4:17

For this light momentary affliction is preparing for us an eternal weight of glory beyond all comparison.

DECREE FOR TODAY: We decree that we will dwell in the Secret Place with God! No demon can enter that!

Father, in Jesus' Name, thank you for hearing our prayers and giving ear to our supplications. Help us to meditate on your doings and ponder the works of your hands for they are many and mighty Lord! We give you glory! We lean and trust in you, Lord. Help us to walk in your ways. We lift up our inner selves to you! Your righteousness keeps our lives out of trouble and free from stress. Thank you, Lord! Thank you for being our Rock and our strength! You are our steadfast love, our fortress, our high tower and our deliverer. You are our shield. We trust in you and take refuge. Every day we will bless you and meditate on your wondrous works. In Jesus' Name, we thank you Lord!

MARCH 13

James 5:11

Behold, we consider those blessed who remained steadfast. You have heard of the steadfastness of Job, and you have seen the purpose of the Lord, how the Lord is compassionate and merciful.

DECREE FOR TODAY: We decree that the Master of the Universe, JESUS, is in control in your home, on the job, wherever we are! Fear not what we have to face today! God has gone before us!

Father, in Jesus' Name, we come humbly and yet boldly to your throne today because you have given us permission to do so. We honor you, Lord! There is no one like you; nothing absolutely nothing can compare to your love. Your word declares that we can have peace and confidence in you; and in this world, there will be much tribulation, trials and frustration but you told us to be of good cheer, you have overcome the world! Great is your faithfulness! Lord, you fashioned the members of our bodies, yet when there was none of them. Oh how powerful you are, Lord. Your thoughts are precious to us! Search our hearts, and if there is any wickedness in us, remove it, Lord. Thank you for blotting out our sins. Help us not to let our good be evil spoken of. Help us to have pure motives. Surely the righteous shall give thanks unto you and dwell in your presence. In Jesus' Name, we thank you!

MARCH 14

Revelation 21:4

He will wipe away every tear from their eyes, and death shall be no more, neither shall there be mourning, nor crying, nor pain anymore, for the former things have passed away.

DECREE FOR TODAY: We decree that on this day we will say thank you Lord! Whatever happens, whatever it is, say thank you Lord! Glory to God!

Father, in Jesus' Name, thank you for this great plan of salvation that equips us to escape eternal destruction. Oh, how wonderful you are. There is none like you in heaven nor in the earth. You do the impossible. You pull us out of situations that are set up to destroy our characters, our minds, and our determination to push forward. Thank you, Lord God! We are grateful for the blood of Jesus that has taken away the power of the adversary over mankind. Glory to God! Grateful for the endurance you have placed within us to face every obstacle, utilizing the faith you have placed within us that causes us to be fully persuaded that you can do absolutely anything. We bless you, Lord, for keeping the air purified and keeping our memories for years and years. Lord God, you are mighty. We rest in you, knowing that today, tomorrow and the rest of our lives are within your hands, the God that created us for your glory. In Jesus' Name, we thank you Lord!

MARCH 15

Psalms 34:18

The LORD is nigh unto them that are of a broken heart; and saveth such as be of a contrite spirit.

DECREE FOR TODAY: We decree that we will not be tossed to and fro and carried by every wind and doctrine

Father, in Jesus' Name, we are grateful for your love, your compassion, your long-suffering, mercy and grace that you have extended to your people. We praise you for looking beyond our faults and seeing our needs. Worthy is the Lamb to be praised. Thank for strength to go forward. Thank you for seeing worthiness in your people to preserve us from destruction. Thank you for being consistent with your love. Oh, how wonderful you are, Lord. We give you glory! Bless the children today, God. Keep them safe in the schools, on the streets, and wherever they are located. Direct their steps. Bless those that are hurting because of situations created around them. Bless the people that are crying inside but laughing outside. Thank you for you promise to bring down high places and make the crooked places straight. In Jesus' Name, we thank you Lord!

MARCH 16

Psalms 51:17

The sacrifices of God [are] a broken spirit: a broken and a contrite heart, O God, thou wilt not despise.

DECREE FOR TODAY: We decree that we will stand! Having done all, we will STAND!

Father, in Jesus' Name, we bless you for another day, Lord. We honor your goodness and favor towards your people. You are Lord over all. Nothing is beyond your control. Thank you for the power that you possess over mankind that keeps us in the most corrupt atmospheres that we find ourselves in. Glory to your Name. We thank you for the power that is in the Name of Jesus that breaks every rock, breaks every stronghold, breaks every yoke, pulls down everything, every imagination, and every evil thought that exalts itself against us. Hallelujah! Thank you that we can depend on you. There is no failure in you. We lay our cares before you,

Lord, for you said cast them unto you! Thank you. We pray for peace in families, unity, and restoration. We pray for those that are hurting and wounded; some seem wounded beyond repair. But you are the God of restoration. Thank you Lord, in Jesus' Name!

MARCH 17

Isaiah 57:15

For thus saith the high and lofty One that inhabiteth eternity, whose name [is] Holy; I dwell in the high and holy [place], with him also [that is] of a contrite and humble spirit, to revive the spirit of the humble, and to revive the heart of the contrite ones.

DECREE FOR TODAY: We decree that we will not fear, nor be dismayed! We know that God is with us! Tell the devil it is so!

Father, in Jesus' Name, we praise you for sitting high and looking low, beholding all of our goings! Thank you for covering us daily from the unkind atmosphere that is sometimes created around us, Lord. We give you glory. Thank you for shutting the mouths of the gainsayers. Thank you for the strength to rise above and quench every dart that is sent our way, regardless of the sender. You sit in high places. You hear all things! Nothing takes you by surprise. Thank you for the unction that you have put within your people to guide and direct us so that we don't fall into the trap nor are we ignorant of Satan's devices. Hallelujah! We bless you, Lord! We praise you for putting a praise within us that will lift us above everything that comes to attack our minds. Thank you for making us more than conquerors! In Jesus' Name!

MARCH 18

John 12:24

Verily, verily, I say unto you, Except a corn of wheat fall into the ground and die, it abideth alone: but if it die, it bringeth forth much fruit.

DECREE FOR TODAY: We decree that greater is coming!

Father, in Jesus' Name, thank you! Thank you for being God in our lives. Thank you for the anointing that breaks every yoke. Thank you for loving us. Thank you for making a way out of no way. We honor you, Lord. We press towards the greater that is in us, giving us authority over everything that is not like you, giving us power to call those things that are not as though they be, giving us hope in situations that seem hopeless, and giving us strength to keep going when it looks like a dead end! We give you glory, Lord. Thank you for lifting the bowed down heads. You do the miraculous! You do the impossibilities. You turn man's "no" into "yes"! Thank you God! We stand in the gap for those that can't pray for themselves for whatever they may be going through that is heavy. We lift them up, Lord. We will praise you on their behalf. Send your glory to them today, Lord. In Jesus' Name, we thank you!

MARCH 19

Proverbs 3:5-6

Trust in the LORD with all thine heart; and lean not unto thine own understanding.

DECREE FOR TODAY: We decree that we will not allow or hearts to be hardened by the things we must endure!

Father, in Jesus' Name, we are grateful, oh so grateful to wake up again in the land of the living. You didn't allow us to sleep on into eternity but gave all of us another opportunity to see your glory, to feel your presence, and to get our lives in order, where needed. Hallelujah! Thank you for maintaining our cause, and for sitting on the throne and judging righteously. Glory to God! Thank you for being a stronghold for the oppressed, in the time of trouble. Your words are pure like silver refined in the earth. We stand on your word! We trust you, Lord, in spite of our circumstances, and in spite of what today or tomorrow may bring. Our help cometh from the Lord! Those that have acquaintance with your mercy will lean on and confidently put their trust in you. All of your promises are yea and amen! Not one faileth! In Jesus' Name, we thank you Lord!

MARCH 20

<u>Psalms 31:12</u>
I am forgotten as a dead man out of mind: I am like a broken vessel.

DECREE FOR TODAY: We decree that we shall live and not die! We will walk in our victory today as children of the Most High God!

Father, in Jesus' Name, great is thy faithfulness unto us! Great is your mercy and your compassions fail not! Regardless of what is going on in the earth, you are the King of the earth, our strong tower, our battle-axe, our deliverer, our source and whatever else we need. We are complete in you, Lord. It is in you that we live and move and have our being! We thank you for keeping us and helping us to live righteously, for in this flesh dwelleth no good thing. Without you, we would be hopeless, wandering around without purpose, without direction! Take us through this day, Lord, and make the devil behave. Lock the hands of the demonic forces on their way to do evil on the job and in the home. We thank you for it, in Jesus' Name!

MARCH 21

<u>2 Corinthians 1:8-10</u>
For we would not, brethren, have you ignorant of our trouble which came to us in Asia, that we were pressed out of measure, above strength, insomuch that we despaired even of life.

DECREE FOR TODAY: We decree that God has spoken good things concerning us! Tell the devil it is so!

Father, in Jesus' Name, thank you being the Mighty God. The Great I AM is present in the earth. Hallelujah! Thank you that our trials make us stronger, make us trust you more, Lord; cause us to see your miraculous works in our lives. Glory to God! We praise you for the power of the Holy Ghost that puts us in control of our minds, our surroundings, our encounters and guarantees us victory. We are more than conquerors through you. Help us to daily operate under your anointing, for it will break every yoke! Thank you for peace, love and joy in our hearts. Lord, many are going through rough places, but you promised that we would go through the waters and you will be with us, through the rivers and you won't let them overwhelm us nor will you allow the fire to burn us. We will stand. We won't take down! We won't go back! We will fight this good fight of faith through you, Lord, in Jesus' Name!

MARCH 22

James 4:6

But he giveth more grace. Wherefore he saith, God resisteth the proud, but giveth grace unto the humble.

DECREE FOR TODAY: We decree that we will stand fast in this liberty wherein Christ has set us free! We will NOT be bound on the job, in the home, wherever! Tell the devil it is so!!

Father, in Jesus' Name, thank you for being our Jehovah Jireh, our provider. In the presence of Jehovah is peace, joy and divine protection. Thank you that your eyes are running to and fro in the earth beholding all the good and the evil. Thank you for the angels that you have dispatched to watch over your people. We love you, Lord. We appreciate your longsuffering, your grace, your mercy and all that you have given to us so freely. Thank you for this great plan of salvation that keeps us from going astray and keeps us under the blood protection provided by you, Jesus! Thank you for monitoring our thoughts and not allowing us to put into action those things that are contrary to your thoughts. Oh, how marvelous is your power, Lord. Your thoughts are not like ours and your ways are not like ours. Thank you for the plan to give us an expected end. In Jesus' Name, we thank you Lord!

MARCH 23

Acts 20:24

But none of these things move me, neither count I my life dear unto myself, so that I might finish my course with joy, and the ministry, which I have received of the Lord Jesus, to testify the gospel of the grace of God.

DECREE FOR TODAY: We decree that nothing can separate us from the love of God – no demon, no enemy, no family, no test nor trial!

Father, in Jesus' Name, thank you for the gift of life. We honor you for your faithfulness, Lord. There is none like you. You are the lifter of the bowed down head. We pray for those that are feeling heavy today. And, Lord, some are feeling like Job felt when he said if his grief was ever weighed, it would be heavier than the sands of the sea. He lacked words to express his grief. But, Lord, the glory is that you blessed him with twice as much as he lost because he trusted you and said though you slay him, yet would he trust in you. We trust you today. Strengthen your people where strength is needed. Dry the tears of those that are weeping outwardly and inwardly. You have purpose in everything that touches our lives. We speak victory for your word declares that we are more than conquerors! In Jesus' Name, we thank you Lord!

MARCH 24

Matthew 5:3-4

Blessed [are] the poor in spirit: for theirs is the kingdom of heaven.

DECREE FOR TODAY: We decree that our God is greater in us than he that is in the world! He said it!

Father, in Jesus' Name, thank you for loving us. Without you we would be hopeless in a corrupt and evil world, Lord. Thank you for sustaining us, even as we dwell in these houses of clay whose foundations are in the dust. Glory to God! Thank you for the great and unsearchable, marvelous things that you do without number. You speak and it rains upon the earth. Everything has to obey you. You sit high those that be low and those that mourn are exalted to safety. That's your word, Lord, and we receive it. Daily you disappoint the devices of the clever so that their hands cannot perform anything against us that will prosper. Thank you, God! You have promised that in famine, you will keep your people from death. Thank you for your provisions, Lord! In Jesus' Name!

MARCH 25

Psalms 51:1

Have mercy upon me, O God, according to thy lovingkindness: according unto the multitude of thy tender mercies blot out my transgressions.

DECREE FOR TODAY: We decree that our light affliction, which is but for a moment, works for us a far more exceeding and eternal weight of glory! This too will pass!

Father, in Jesus' Name, thank you for the gift of life! We have been crucified with you, Lord, and the lives that we now live are no longer us but you that lives within us! Glory! We are living by faith, Lord, completely trusting and relying upon you. There is no other! We won't ignore this wonderful gift of grace, your unmerited favor that you have bestowed upon us. You have purpose in each of us. Help us to fulfill your calling without doubt but with assurance that this good work that you have begun in your people you will fulfill it until the day of Christ. We are coming boldly to your throne to obtain help in the time of need. Thank you for the privilege. Bless your people today with health, jobs, strength, endurance and determination not to quit, but to wait on you, Lord! Weeping may endure for the night but thank you for the joy that you will surely send. In Jesus' Name, we thank you!

MARCH 26

1 John 1:9

If we confess our sins, he is faithful and just to forgive us [our] sins, and to cleanse us from all unrighteousness.

DECREE: We decree that a soft answer turneth away wrath! We will hold our tongues in Jesus' Name!

Father, in Jesus' Name, thank you for refreshing us, refreshing our spirits, our anointing, our minds and all that pertains to us. Without you we would be useless, Lord. We bless you for the comfort you give to your people in an uncomfortable world. Thank you for giving us strength to endure painful and disappointing situations and turning them around to bless us. Glory to God! We praise you for the freedom to worship you. Thank you for the ability to search for you with all of our hearts and to find you! Thank you Jesus! You favor your people. Let your blessings run us down and overtake us. You promised to make your people the head and not the tail. We know that all of your promises are yea and amen. We believe it, we receive it, and our expectations are of you, Lord. We thank you, in Jesus' Name!

MARCH 27

Isaiah 66:1-2

Thus saith the LORD, The heaven [is] my throne, and the earth [is] my footstool: where [is] the house that ye build unto me? and where [is] the place of my rest?

DECREE FOR TODAY: We decree that this joy that we have, the world didn't give it to us and the world can't take it away. Tell the devil it is so!

Father, in the Name of Jesus thank you for rest in the soul, in the spirit, and in the mind! You have blessed us with peace that passeth all understanding. Thank you for that gift of peace, Lord, that is available to your people. Thank you, Lord, that we can cry unto you and be delivered. We can trust in you and never be disappointed or ashamed. We rely on you, Lord, with confidence and steadfastness. Your compassions and your lovingkindness, they fail not. Our weeping may endure for a night, but joy is coming in the morning. We have your word, Lord! The petitions that are before you, we will wait confidently for you. We will be strong. Having done all, we will STAND and see the salvation of the Lord in Jesus' Name, we thank you!

MARCH 28

Romans 8:28

And we know that God causes all things to work together for good to those who love God, to those who are called according to His purpose.

DECREE FOR TODAY: We decree that surely the Lord will deliver us from ALL of our afflictions!

Father, in Jesus' Name, thank you for keeping us through our nights. Lord, many are feeling down and out, many are ready to throw in the towel because of the cares of this life, and many just don't know what to do Lord. But, we thank you that you have left your word here that says when we pass through the waters, you will be with us; And through the rivers, they will not overwhelm us. When we walk through fire, we will not be scorched, nor will the flame burn us. Glory to God! We believe your word, Lord! We rebuke every demonic force that is speaking to the minds of your people. We take authority over every discouraging, aggravating and annoying spirit floating in the atmosphere! We are going to wait on you, Lord, for you are a due time God! Nothing is too hard for you and you are sure to perform your promises. We thank you for it, in Jesus' Name!

MARCH 29

John 14:27
Peace I leave with you; My peace I give to you; not as the world gives do I give to you. Do not let your heart be troubled, nor let it be fearful.

DECREE FOR TODAY: We decree that we will fear NO man! We will walk, not in pride, but in power in the Name of Jesus!

Father, in Jesus' Name, thank you for being our Rock and our fortress. All that we need is in you, Lord. Many are going through difficult, rough times but through it all, we learn how to trust you. And like Job, when you are allowing us to go through our tests, yet will we trust you! We will continue to look unto the hills from whence cometh our help. Our strength depends on your strength, Lord. Help us to remember that our purpose in his earth is to be pleasing to you. Our motives in what we do must meet your approval. Thank you for guiding us into all truth. In spite of what life brings, we will be rooted, grounded and established in you and in your word, Lord! Your word is food unto our souls. We won't be weary nor faint for you have given us the power to cross our Red Seas, our Jordan Rivers, and to stand still until our Jericho Walls are brought down with a shout. Thank you Lord, in Jesus' Name!

MARCH 30

Isaiah 41:10
Do not fear, for I am with you; Do not anxiously look about you, for I am your God I will strengthen you, surely I will help you, Surely I will uphold you with My righteous right hand.

DECREE FOR TODAY: We decree that we will hold our peace! The Lord shall fight for us.

Father, in the Name of Jesus we say thank you! We celebrate your death and resurrection, we say Glory, we say Hallelujah, and we say thank you for taking the stripes for us! Thank you for allowing those that beat you to carry out their mission. Glory to God! Where would we be had you not gone through it all, Lord? We bless you. We honor you. Help us to live up to the value and appreciation of the Cross. Help us to love one another and be kind to each other. Help us to be especially kind to the children and parents. Mend broken relationships, Lord. Touch the hearts of your people that are feeling troubled. You are the lifter upper of the bowed down head. You are the Rock that cannot be broken. You are our Comforter. We bless you today, Lord; and we thank you for this moment - this moment that is putting us closer to your coming, in Jesus' Name!

MARCH 31

Psalm 23:4

Even though I walk through the valley of the shadow of death, I fear no evil, for You are with me; Your rod and Your staff, they comfort me.

DECREE FOR TODAY: We decree that we will not despise small things! Greater is coming! Tell it to yourself and believe it!

Father, in Jesus' Name, we thank you that our groanings and our desires are before you. Your lovingkindness is better than life. Your mercy and grace are so precious to us, Lord. Thank you for preplanning ways to help us overcome every obstacle. We bless you, Lord. Help us to desire your divine will, not your permissive will, for our lives. Thank you for leaving the Word of God here for us to bring us hope. Thank you that we can stand still in every battle and come out victoriously, for the battle belongs to you and not us. We can run and not become weary. We can walk and not faint because your word puts strength in us. Just hearing your word works miracles in our lives – renews us, lifts our spirits, gives us joy! Glory to God. In Jesus' Name, we thank you!

APRIL 1

Proverbs 3:5-6

Trust in the LORD with all your heart And do not lean on your own understanding. In all your ways acknowledge Him, And He will make your paths straight.

DECREE FOR TODAY: We decree that we are kept by the power of God through faith unto salvation. Nothing can pluck us out of the hand of God! Tell the devil it is so!

Father, in Jesus' Name, we honor your presence. Oh, how blessed we are to be able to have the God of the Universe living inside of us, loving us, directing us, protecting us and providing all of our needs. Thank you God! What a privilege it is to be able to call on the Almighty, the All Power, in our times of need and get answers. Hallelujah! We pray for peace for your people today, Lord, that have been disturbed by the things of this life. We take authority over our space in our minds, on the jobs, in the homes, and wherever we may be. We refuse to allow the negativity of this world to overcome us. We won't be shaken Lord. We will STAND, in spite of what the day brings. Our today, tomorrow and forever are in your hands, not the hands of men. We won't forget that mercy and grace are hanging in the atmosphere for us. Your thoughts and plans towards us are good and not evil and to give us an expected end. Thank you Lord, in Jesus' Name!

APRIL 2

Matthew 5:4

Blessed are those who mourn, for they shall be comforted.

DECREE FOR TODAY: We decree that God is our ROCK! We will not turn to the right nor to the left!

Father, in the Name of Jesus we give you glory today, Lord. We are assured of victory. Thank you for you are our strength, our personal bravery and our invisible army. Glory to God. Thank you that you don't allow us to fear as we walk through the terror of this life, but you have given us power to stand against the wiles of the devil! Thank you, Lord. You are our Rock, our refuge and shield, our stronghold. Thank you for saving us from violence. We lift up our eyes to the hills from whence cometh our help for our help comes from the Lord. We bind the strong man today, Lord. We take authority over the atmosphere and nothing shall separate us from your love! Glory to God! We are new creatures in you, molded and created in your image. Thank you for putting your power in these earthen vessels; though we are just clay, the dust of the earth, your power has made us strong enough to endure every type of storm spiritually and physically. Thank you Lord, in Jesus' Name!

APRIL 3

<u>Revelation 21:4</u>

He will wipe away every tear from their eyes; and there will no longer be any death; there will no longer be any mourning, or crying, or pain; the first things have passed away.

DECREE FOR TODAY: We decree that we will guard our ways that we may not sin with our tongues.

Father, in Jesus' Name, thank you for the peace of God that passeth all understanding that keeps our hearts and our minds through you, Lord. We don't honor you enough for keeping our minds, but today we say thank you for not letting us forget things, helping us to maintain memory so that we don't wander around. Grateful to you, Lord. And we pray for those that have lost memory, Lord. You are a restorer! Yes you are! We won't be anxious today, Lord. We will be content. We won't allow our minds to be disrupted by the things going on in this world. We will think on things that are honest, just, pure, lovely and of a good report. We will think on these things and give you praise, Lord! Hallelujah! We will let go and let God be God, in Jesus' Name!

APRIL 4

<u>Matthew 11:28</u>

Come to Me, all who are weary and heavy-laden, and I will give you rest.

DECREE FOR TODAY: We decree that we have the favor of God! Nothing can happen to us without God's permission and if he allows it, he will bring us through it!

Father, in the Name of Jesus, we honor your Name, Lord. There's no other name given under heaven whereby we shall be saved other than the Name of Jesus! Thank you, Lord, that your Name is a strong tower and the righteous runneth into it and is safe. Thank you for covering us as we sleep, Lord, keeping our minds intact, and keeping the blood running through our veins without human assistance. Glory to God. You keep us breathing day by day. We don't take it lightly! Thank you for the air! Thank you for purifying it so that we can continue to function. Thank you for the ability to read your word, hear it and the power you have invested in us to obey it. Thank you for your protection for when the enemy comes in like a flood, the spirit of the Lord lifts up a standard against him in the home, on the job, and wherever we are! Hallelujah! In Jesus' Name, we thank you Lord!

APRIL 5

Psalm 18:2

The LORD is my rock and my fortress and my deliverer, My God, my rock, in whom I take refuge; My shield and the horn of my salvation, my stronghold.

DECREE FOR TODAY: We decree that grace and mercy are following us! Tell the devil it is so and he has no power over it!

Father, in Jesus' Name, thank you for this great day that you have spared our lives once again. Glory to God! Thank you that every weapon formed against us shall not prosper. Thank you that ever crooked place will be made smooth and every mountain must come down. Thank you for faith that is so powerful that it will move mountains. Thank you for grace, your unmerited favor towards us. We bless you, Lord! We pray for every soul reading this prayer and their families. We pray for peace and prosperity. We pray your blessings will overtake them. We pray for strength and renewed minds. We lift our hands in praise to you, Lord, knowing that whatever is not is place will be and whatever happens, you are in control. We rest in you, Lord, knowing you can handle anything. We thank you for the blood of Jesus, in Jesus' Name!

APRIL 6

John 16:33

These things I have spoken to you, so that in Me you may have peace In the world you have tribulation, but take courage; I have overcome the world.

DECREE FOR TODAY: We decree that the Lord is God of all flesh and there is nothing too hard for him! Give him some glory!

Father, in Jesus' Name, thank you for the determination to go forward, to move from the now to what you have planned for us. We are determined to make it, to overcome obstacles, fear, doubt, enemies and whatever we have to face! We are going to use your strength, Lord, to push us to the destiny you designed for us from the foundation of the world. No demon can stop us. You are unstoppable. Our help comes from you, Lord, your sanctuary! Thank you, God! We praise you for the divine help that is available to us to propel us, even when we don't feel like we can go any further. There is a plan in place prepared by you and we are going to fix our minds on it so that the enemy cannot distract us. Let your anointing flow today, Lord. For the anointing will break every yoke. We receive your help and thank you for it, in Jesus' Name!

APRIL 7

<u>Romans 8:31</u>
What then shall we say to these things? If God is for us, who is against us?

DECREE FOR TODAY: We decree that we will NOT render evil for evil!

Father, in Jesus' Name, thank you for your presence in our lives. Where would we be without you Lord? There is none like you, Lord. You are our Rock. Thank you for your thoughts towards us and your plans towards us which are for our best interest and our peace in this earth and to give us an expected end. Help us to see that your plans work and we need only wait for you. We are grateful for the secret place that you have for us to dwell in from the plots of evil men and women. You understand our thoughts long before they enter our minds. Thank you for managing our thinking, as we yield ourselves to you for directions. In Jesus' Name, we thank you!

APRIL 8

<u>2 Corinthians 1:3-4</u>
Blessed be the God and Father of our Lord Jesus Christ, the Father of mercies and God of all comfort, who comforts us in all our affliction so that we will be able to comfort those who are in any affliction with the comfort with which we ourselves are comforted by God.

DECREE FOR TODAY: We decree that we will remind ourselves this day that we are not wrestling against flesh and blood – not against people –but against the principalities, against powers, against the demonic rulers of darkness of this world!

Father, in Jesus' Name, we thank you! Thank you for the sunshine! Thank you for your blessings in our lives. Thank you for the miraculous things you have done for us. We have all come short of your glory but you keep on pouring out mercy and grace upon us. Hallelujah! Lord you said if we abide in you and your word abide in us, we can ask you anything according to your will and you will do it. We believe it, Lord. Heal that sick body that is waiting for your touch, Lord. Deliver those that are being held captive, those that are in prisons unjustly, deliver them, Lord; and those there justly held captive, extend your mercy and a second chance for the willing heart. Visit the brokenhearted. Mend the broken pieces back together. We rebuke loneliness. We speak comfort to the disturbed in mind. We take hold of this peace that you have given to us that surpasses all understanding. In Jesus' Name, we thank you for the victory in all things!

APRIL 9

Jeremiah 29:11

For I know the plans that I have for you,' declares the LORD, plans for welfare and not for calamity to give you a future and a hope.

DECREE FOR TODAY: We decree that this is the day that the Lord made for us! We will rejoice in it! The devil will NOT take our joy! It's controlled by the mind!

Father, in Jesus' Name, thank for this day! We honor you, Lord! There is none like you. You continue to amaze us with life, provision, healing and making ways out of no ways, opening doors that don't exist, closing doors that you don't want us to enter. Thank you Lord! Your Blood still works, and we thank you Lord! Our hearts are still beating; we are alive! Glory to God! We will praise you while we can! Oh, what a miracle. Thank you for whatever state we are in though for some it may not be the most convenient, your word declares that the steps of a good man are ordered by the Lord. Your word is our guide – thank you that you didn't leave us to our own understanding to wander around hopelessly in this dangerous world. Our hope is in you, our comfort, our healing, our deliverance and everything we need is in you, Lord! We give you glory for being greater inside of us than he that is in the world. In Jesus' Name!

APRIL 10

2 Timothy 1:7

For God has not given us a spirit of timidity, but of power and love and discipline.

DECREE FOR TODAY: We decree that we will not be moved! We refuse to be moved, even in the mind! We will STAND still and see the salvation of the Lord!

Father, in Jesus' Name, thank you for this great plan of salvation. Thank you for mapping out our lives before the foundation of the world. We pray for those that are struggling, trying to figure out what to do to handle difficult situations. We pray that they will get to know that you have already figured everything out. We need only to obey you, and you promised that our blessings will overtake us, in due time. Thank you for planting the feet of your people so that if we acknowledge you, you will direct our paths. Help us not to despise suffering; after that we have suffered a while, you will make us perfect, stablish, strengthen, and settle us. Help us to let steadfastness have its full effect in our lives. All things are working together for our good. That's your word. Having done all, we will stand! Nothing can be compared to the things you have in store for your people. We thank you for it in Jesus' Name!

APRIL 11

Romans 5:5

And hope does not disappoint, because the love of God has been poured out within our hearts through the Holy Spirit who was given to us.

DECREE FOR TODAY: We decree that God has made us kings and priests. We will not be belittled by any man! Tell the devil it is written!

Father, in Jesus' Name, thank you! Thank you! Thank you, God! Hallelujah! You are worthy of our praises. We owe you sacrifices of praise. You have given us the garment of praise for the spirit of heaviness. We pray for release for those feeling bound and as though they have no hope. You are great in the earth. Your power still surpasses all power. Your love for us is unmeasurable. Sometimes, Lord, we forget where you have brought us from, and we focus on the now situations. But had it not been for the Lord on our side, where would we be? You have carried us through storms and things that seemed as though they would have drowned us, but you sustained us. You strengthened us! Help us not to forget. We have your promise that all things are working for our good. No weapon formed against us shall prosper. In you we live, we move and have our being. We shall live and not die! Victory belongs to your children. We thank you for it Lord in Jesus' Name!

APRIL 12

Psalm 55:22

Cast your burden upon the LORD and He will sustain you; He will never allow the righteous to be shaken.

DECREE FOR TODAY: We decree that we will not walk in the counsel of the ungodly! Tell the devil it is so!

Father, in Jesus' Name, thank you for the Blessed Hope that lies within us. Your Name is a strong tower, we can run into it and be safe! Glory to God! We will rejoice in this Hope. We will be constant in prayer and patient in tribulation by the grace of God! We remember that your plans for us are good and not evil and to give us an expected end. We will rejoice in our sufferings, knowing that suffering produces endurance, and our endurance produces a good character, which gives us hope, Lord God. And Hope does not put us to shame. Glory to God! We refuse to be weary, Lord. We will run and not allow weariness to overtake us! We won't faint, Lord. We know that you will renew our strength! That's your word! We believe it. We receive it and we declare it to be so, in Jesus' Name!

APRIL 13

Psalm 46:1

God is our refuge and strength, A very present help in trouble.

DECREE FOR TODAY: We decree that we will submit ourselves to God, resist the devil and he WILL flee! Tell the devil it is so!

Father, in Jesus' Name, thank you for this moment in time that you have so freely given to your people, whether we serve you or disobey you – you have given us a choice. Thank you, God, for this great gift of life, this opportunity to experience your glory, and this wonderful time of refreshing in the Spirit! We've come short of your glory; but, God, you still shower us with love, with provisions, and with revelations. Glory to God! Thank you for the earth that drinks in the rain and brings forth food to keep us alive - Thank you, God! Thank for the tears, though sometime painful to us, you said weeping may endure for a night, but joy cometh in the morning. Hallelujah! We will hold the beginning of our confidence steadfast unto the end, Lord. Come what may! Our God reigns! Our God is victorious in every battle! Our God will fight for us spiritually, mentally, and naturally! Whatever it is, the battle belongs to God! It is not ours! Thank you for that, Lord, in Jesus' Name!

APRIL 14

Nahum 1:7

The LORD is good, A stronghold in the day of trouble, And He knows those who take refuge in Him.

DECREE FOR TODAY: We decree that come what may, our confidence in God will still remain! Tell the devil it is so!

Father, in Jesus' Name, thank you for drawing us into your Kingdom. As we have received you, Lord, we will walk in your word. We will conform to the lifestyle you designed for us. Through your power, and no goodness of our own, we will conduct ourselves according to your Word! We will continue to build up ourselves in you, Lord, being rooted and grounded in you and established in the faith. Help us to let the peace of God rule in our lives daily. Help us to have the mind of Christ so that our minds will remain in a peaceful state. Thank you for this Blessed Hope that lives within us, Lord. We will wait and hope for you with expectation. We will be of a good courage. We won't let our hearts be troubled, Lord – fearing nothing! For, lo, you are with us. We won't be terrified nor dismayed by the things we see. You are our God! We thank you for it, in Jesus' Name!

APRIL 15

Psalm 30:5

For His anger is but for a moment, His favor is for a lifetime; Weeping may last for the night, But a shout of joy comes in the morning.

DECREE FOR TODAY: We decree that we will not allow our minds to be filled with things that don't matter! Tell the devil not today!

Father, in the Name of Jesus, we love you, Lord. We adore you. We stand in awe of you, your great power, your creation and your wisdom that you have imparted to mankind. Glory to God! Father, as we go about our daily goings, most times we fail to tell you thank you for the little things that keep us going. My My, Lord. Oh, what wisdom you have. Thanking you for our eyes to see, our ability to feel and taste. Lord Jesus, we give you glory. And, something as small as our big toes that you designed, we cover them up and we don't think too much about them, but without them we would lose our balance. Grateful today for small things, small beginnings. Grateful that we have food to eat. Help us not to be wasteful. We lift our hands and say Hallelujah! Hallelujah! Our God reigns in the earth and in us. In Jesus' Name, we thank you Lord!

APRIL 16

Psalm 73:26

My flesh and my heart may fail, But God is the strength of my heart and my portion forever.

DECREE FOR TODAY: We decree that we will cease from anger – for he that is slow to anger is better than the mighty and he that ruleth his spirit than he that taketh a city!

Father, in Jesus' Name, thank you for being our strong habitation. You are our Rock! You are our refuge! Let the spirit of prayer fall upon us. Let there be a revival in the land, in our homes, and in us! Glory to God! Renew us. Take us to a new level in you. Help us to rise above the now and see through your eyes that all things are in place. Every problem has already been solved. Everything we need has already been given. Let us see them manifested in our lives now, Lord. We are, through your power, calling those things that are not as though they were. We are declaring victory in every situation. We speak wholeness. We speak provision. We speak revelations. We declare that all things that concern us are working for our good! We rest in you Lord. We are declaring that our morning is now. No more delay! We thank you for the miraculous things that we will experience in the days to come. We receive them, in Jesus' Name!

APRIL 17

<u>1 Peter 5:7</u>

Casting all your anxiety on Him, because He cares for you.

DECREE FOR TODAY: We decree that no good thing will the Lord withhold from us if we walk upright!

Father, in Jesus' Name, great is thy faithfulness unto us! Lord, when we have not been faithful, you have remained the same. Thank you for not changing. Thank you for being the same yesterday, today and forever! Glory to God! We are setting our affections on things that are above and not on things that are on this earth! We are dead to ourselves and our life is hid with Christ in you, Father, We acknowledge who you are, Lord. The Great I AM. The Father, in creation. Lord, thank you for creating a body for yourself and naming yourself, Jesus! Glory to God. For there is no other name under heaven given among men whereby we can be saved. Hallelujah! We call your Name, JESUS, in our homes, on our jobs, and in every situation! JESUS! Hallelujah! Thank you for walking the earth. You can relate to our earthly trials. Glory to God. Thank for being touched by our infirmities. We will continue in prayer and watch, with thanksgiving. In Jesus' Name, we thank you!

APRIL 18

<u>Psalm 16:8</u>

I have set the LORD continually before me; Because He is at my right hand, I will not be shaken.

DECREE FOR TODAY: We decree that we will fear no evil! God is with us! Tell the devil God said so!

Father, in Jesus' Name, thank for this day, Lord God! We worship you Lord! We give you all the glory! Hallelujah! We don't know what today will bring, but we say thank you because how precious are your thoughts towards us! Man cannot number them. They are good and to give us an expected end. Father, we pray for the body of Christ. We pray for homes and relationships that are disturbed. We pray for children that are in those homes, Lord. We speak peace. Lord, many are ready to throw in the towel. But, you have given us power over the enemy! We declare righteousness to prevail in homes. We bind up everything that is hindering your people that are crying out to you. We take authority over the atmosphere. We command the forces of darkness to flee, in the Name of Jesus. We apply the blood to our lives, for you have already made us conquerors. Help us to hide that in our minds, Lord. We thank you, in Jesus' Name!

APRIL 19

Romans 8:18

For I consider that the sufferings of this present time are not worthy to be compared with the glory that is to be revealed to us.

DECREE FOR TODAY: We decree that it is better to trust in the Lord than to put confidence in man!

Father, in Jesus' Name, thank you for all things – every trial, every test, every tear drop, every persecution, every evil word spoken against us, every plot, and every activity that has tried to dethrone the hope in the minds of your people. For it is through suffering that we get to know you, even as Paul did through the fellowship of your suffering. Glory to God! Regardless of how we look or feel, we are reigning in power, the power that you have invested in us! We don't walk proudly or boasting but in display of your divine favor rewarded for obedience. Thank you, Lord! We have all come short, but your forgiveness is unmeasurable! Your toleration has extended beyond our comprehension. Thank you for mercy, Lord! We bless you today for you are our God, and there is none other! In Jesus' Name, we thank you, Lord!

APRIL 20

Isaiah 12:2

Behold, God is my salvation, I will trust and not be afraid; For the LORD GOD is my strength and song, And He has become my salvation.

DECREE FOR TODAY: We decree that Being confident of this very thing, that he which hath begun a good work in you will perform it until the day of Jesus Christ! Tell the devil it is so!

Father, in Jesus' Name, thank you for preserving us! We put our trust in you, Lord! You are the portion of our inheritance. We bless you. Thank you for giving us counsel and instructions. We won't be moved, Lord. We will rejoice in you, for in your presence is the fullness of joy! Thank you that your eyes are open unto the righteous and you hear their cries and delivereth them out of all of their troubles! It's your word, Lord. You honor your word. You are nigh to those that be of a broken heart and you save those that are crushed in spirit. Glory to God! We rest in you, Lord. We cast all of our cares upon you for your word declares that all of your promises are yea and amen in Christ! We thank you for it, in Jesus' Name!

APRIL 21

Isaiah 43:2

When you pass through the waters, I will be with you; And through the rivers, they will not overflow you. When you walk through the fire, you will not be scorched, Nor will the flame burn you.

DECREE FOR TODAY: We decree that we will be happy and not walk in the counsel of the ungodly!

Father, in Jesus' Name, thank you for being our God, this God that is our God forever, even unto the end of each of our lives. Thank you, Lord, for helping us to make wise decisions. You said, if we acknowledge you in all of our ways, you will direct our paths. Thank you for being our guide and being that still small voice that says, this is the way, walk ye in it. Glory to God! We exalt you Lord! Thank you for daily supplying our needs. Thank you for taking over our prayers and making intercession for us when we don't know what to pray for. Thank you for preserving us when we go in and when we come out in this world of confusion and corruption. Oh, how you keep us, Lord! Hallelujah! Thank you for making the seas and rivers obey your voice and not overflow and drown us, Lord. Oh, the power that is in our God is unmeasurable. Thank you for the love, Lord, in Jesus' Name!

APRIL 22

John 14:1-3

Do not let your heart be troubled; believe in God, believe also in Me. In My Father's house are many dwelling places; if it were not so, I would have told you; for I go to prepare a place for you. If I go and

prepare a place for you, I will come again and receive you to Myself, that where I am, there you may be also.

DECREE FOR TODAY: We decree that we have put our hands to the plough and we will NOT look back! For if we look back, we are not fit for the kingdom!

Father, in Jesus' Name, we bless you, Lord! We are grateful for your love! We rejoice in you, we praise you, we give you all the glory for dying for us. Hallelujah! No one can pluck us out of your hands! Your eyes run to and fro in the earth beholding the good and the evil. Thank you for your great plans for us and your thoughts towards us for they are good and not evil but to give us an expected end! Thank you for refreshing our spirits day after day, Lord. Thank you for never sleeping but keeping watch over your creation. Thank you for the angelic beings you have assigned to us to watch over us. Glory to God! In your Name, Jesus, we thank you Lord!

APRIL 23

2 Corinthians 12:9

And He has said to me, "My grace is sufficient for you, for power is perfected in weakness" Most gladly, therefore, I will rather boast about my weaknesses, so that the power of Christ may dwell in me.

DECREE FOR TODAY: We decree that when God has tried us – allowed us to go through, we shall come forth as pure gold! Job did! So will we!

Father, in Jesus' Name, we come humbly in reverence and yet in boldness before your throne because of the privilege you have given to us that allows us access to your presence. Glory to God. We are walking in our victory, Lord, and in the anointing, pulling down everything that exalts itself against us. Grateful for this power that you have freely given to your people. We will be rooted and built up in you, Lord, and stablished in the faith. We won't allow any man to spoil us through philosophy and vain deceit after the traditions of men, but we will walk in truth and in the liberty wherein you have set us free from the powers of darkness. We will dwell in your presence, in the secret place! We will hide our feelings and our hearts in the Holy Ghost so that we won't be moved by the fiery darts that come our way! Thank you, Lord, for power to overcome, power to walk on the serpent's head, power to speak to our mountains and they must come down, power to plead the blood of Jesus over every situation and watch each one change for the better. Thank you, Lord, in Jesus' Name!

APRIL 24

<u>Psalm 9:9</u>

The LORD also will be a stronghold for the oppressed, A stronghold in times of trouble.

DECREE FOR TODAY: We decree that greater is he that is within you than he that is in the world! Tell every demon you encounter that God said so!

Father, in Jesus' Name, we will bless the Lord with all that is in us! We give you glory for whatever state we are in. You told us to be content for all things are working together for our good. Lord, you took two fishes and five loaves and fed multitudes, how much more about your people that are looking to you for the miraculous. Open the windows of heaven today, Lord, and pour out a blessing upon your people. Do something supernatural. Lord, many have been waiting for change, for healing, and for turnarounds. We are looking unto you because when you speak, the earth has to obey you and everything that is in it. We thank you for the things that are not because you are the God that can call those things that are not as though they were. We are in expectation of a move of God. Dispatch angels, Lord. Let it be so, Lord, and we thank you for it, in Jesus' Name!

APRIL 25

<u>1 Peter 5:6-7</u>

Therefore humble yourselves under the mighty hand of God, that He may exalt you at the proper time, casting all your anxiety on Him, because He cares for you.

DECREE FOR TODAY: We decree that nothing can separate us from the love of God!

Father, in Jesus' Name, we honor you, the God that created the earth, the sea and everything that is in them by your spoken word, Lord! There is power in the words of our God. Our hope is in you! Thank you for giving food to the hungry and opening blind eyes. Thank you for raising them that are bowed down. Your word declares that you love the righteous. You preserve the strangers. You relieve the fatherless and the widows. You shall reign forever. Help us to hold onto your promises for all of them are yea and amen! To God be the glory! Thank you for restoring our strength and giving power to the faint. You are the God of the NOW! Let your glory be revealed in us, in our speech, and in our tone so that we can give a soft answer that turns away wrath. Thank you Lord, in Jesus' Name!

APRIL 26

Psalm 22:24

For He has not despised nor abhorred the affliction of the afflicted; Nor has He hidden His face from him; But when he cried to Him for help, He heard.

DECREE FOR TODAY: We decree that the devil cannot deceive us for we are not ignorant of his devices!

Father, in Jesus' Name, we thank you for this journey of faith that you have planned for us from the foundation of the world! Thank for the blood of Jesus that has assured of us the victory through faith. Your word declares that if we have the faith the size of a mustard seed we can move mountains. We are using it, Lord – by faith we speak to sick bodies and declare healing! We speak to the weak and declare that they shall be strong. We speak to the minds of those that are ready to throw in the towel and we declare them to be renewed! We command peace in the minds of your people. You have given us peace that surpasses all understanding. We pull it down into the homes of those that are in turmoil. We command the demons of hell to get out of our space, our of our work environments, and out of our families, in the Name of Jesus. By faith, we claim deliverance wherever it is needed, Lord. We thank you for those that will receive it by faith, in Jesus' Name!

APRIL 27

2 Corinthians 5:17

Therefore if anyone is in Christ, he is a new creature; the old things passed away; behold, new things have come.

DECREE FOR TODAY: We decree that if we obey God, according to God's divine will, we can ask him anything and he will do it. Tell the devil God said so!

Father, in Jesus' Name, thank you for salvation. We give you glory, Lord. We acknowledge you for your greatness. We look to you, knowing that the earth is the Lord's and the fullness thereof, knowing that no good thing will you withhold from them that walk uprightly, knowing that all things are working together for our good, knowing that no weapon formed against us shall prosper, knowing that My God shall supply all of our needs according to your riches in glory by Christ Jesus, knowing that many are the afflictions of the righteous but the Lord delivereth them out of them all, knowing that the righteous cry and you hear, knowing that the just shall live by faith, and knowing that you will never leave us nor forsake us! Knowing these things, Glory to God, Lord we say thank you, in Jesus' Name!

APRIL 28

James 1:2

Consider it all joy, my brethren, when you encounter various trials.

DECREE FOR TODAY: We decree that we will trust in the Lord and lean not to our own understanding!

Father, in the Name of Jesus, thank you for Joy. Thank you for the Peace of God that surpasses all understanding. Thank you for the gift of the Holy Ghost that comes to comfort, which comes to teach us, and that comes to keep us until the day of redemption. We glory in your presence. We are going to use this power that you have invested within us to make us think right, to walk on the devil's head, to go forth conquering and coming out victoriously from every battle that has been set before us. For they are your battles. They don't belong to us, Lord. Hallelujah! We realize our bodies are not built to carry worry. Help us to lay aside every weight, regardless of its nature. By faith, we take authority and will overcome everything that is not like you. In Jesus' Name, we thank you Lord!

APRIL 29

<u>Romans 12:12</u>

Rejoicing in hope, persevering in tribulation, devoted to prayer.

DECREE FOR TODAY: We decree that we will bless the Lord at all times. His praise shall continually be in our mouths!

Father, in Jesus' Name, thank you for being the refuge and strength and a very present help in the time of trouble for your people. You are in our midst, we shall not be moved. You are our confidence and we put our trust in you. We have this confidence in you, Lord, that if we ask any thing according to your will you hear us. And if we know that you hear us, whatsoever we ask, we know that we have the petitions that we desire of you! Hallelujah! In the presence of the Lord is strong confidence and your children have a place of refuge. Our eyes are ever toward you, Lord. Be gracious unto us. We have waited for you, Lord. You are our arm every morning, and our salvation in the times of trouble. We are confident of this very thing, that He which hath begun a good work in us will perform it until the day of Jesus Christ. We thank you for it, Lord, in Jesus' Name!

APRIL 30

<u>John 3:16</u>

For God so loved the world, that He gave His only begotten Son, that whoever believes in Him shall not perish, but have eternal life.

DECREE FOR TODAY: I am what God says I am! Declare it in the Name of Jesus! Man's opinion does not determine our destiny!

Father, in Jesus' Name, thank you for bringing us to another day. Oh, how grateful we are that you have spared our lives. You have kept us in our right minds. Glory to God! Great is they faithfulness, Lord. We surrender ourselves to you that you will be able to direct our paths according to your divine will. We pray for those experiencing depression, loneliness and whatever may be causing them to feel down and out during this time that they will look unto the hills from whence cometh our help! You are our source. You have put your Spirit in us to give us power over the devil! Hallelujah! Thank you for the joy. Thank you for the peace. We bless you, Lord, and give you all the glory in Jesus' Name!

MAY 1

Psalm 94:19

When my anxious thoughts multiply within me, Your consolations delight my soul.

DECREE FOR TODAY: We decree that there is power in prayer and what we have asked God for according to his divine will, it SHALL come to pass! Tell the devil God said so!

Father, in Jesus' Name, it is in you that we live, we move, we have our being! Where would we be without you, Lord! You have watched over us as our Shepherd! You have met our needs. You promised that if we seek first the kingdom of God and his righteousness that all of these things will be added unto us. As children of Abraham, by faith, we claim the promise that our blessings will overtake us, if we obey your word! We speak it! We claim it, in the Name of Jesus! Your words says, it is your will that we will prosper and be in good health even as our soul prospers. We claim it. We declare that your word is true! We will stand, we will be still, and we will wait patiently for you. You have promised that in due season we will reap if we faint not! Fainting is not in our spiritual DNA. We rest in the God that lives within us! Lord, your blood still works, it covers, it delivers, and it blots out our sins! Glory to God! We thank you for the covering, Lord, in Jesus' Name!

MAY 2

Psalm 56:3

When I am afraid, I will put my trust in You.

DECREE FOR TODAY: We decree that the Blood still works. We plead the Blood of Jesus against everything that is not like God!

Father, in Jesus' Name, thank you for speaking to our spirits, Lord! There is none like you! I hear victory! I hear overcoming power! I hear deliverance. You said, if your people who are called by your Name will humble ourselves and pray, and seek your face and turn from our wicked ways, you will hear us from heaven, you will forgive us of our sins and will heal the land! Glory to God. Thank you for the renewing of our minds. Thank you for giving us the ability to control our minds. Hallelujah! We can receive or reject what comes to us. What power you have invested in us, Lord. We are not ruled by the powers of darkness of this world! You govern from your authority! There is none like you, God! You have made us priests, royalty, special people and joint heirs with you. We have this rich treasure within us. Help us to realize the value of the power within us. We are walking around with the creator of the world inside! Glory to God! No weapon formed against us shall prosper. We thank you for it, in Jesus' Name!

MAY 3

Psalm 18:28

For You light my lamp; The LORD my God illumines my darkness.

DECREE FOR TODAY: We decree that God has established us and Satan can't move us! Tell the devil God said so!

Father, in Jesus' Name, all of the praises, all of the prayers, all of the thanks combined from the entire world would not be enough to show you our appreciation for your love, Lord! You've kept us! You have brought us through dangers, rough places, mountains that seemed too high, valleys that were low and difficult pit-like situations, but we are all still here! Glory to God! We honor your presence, Lord. Your favor upon the lives of your people is unmeasurable! We are going to trust in you, Lord, with all of our hearts. We won't lean to our own understanding. Your word declares that you, the Lord our God will hold our right hands, saying unto us, Fear not, you will help us. We know that all of your promises are yea and amen! We are casting our burdens upon you; you will sustain your people and NEVER suffer the righteous to be moved. In Jesus' Name, we thank you Lord!

MAY 4

John 14:18

I will not leave you as orphans; I will come to you.

DECREE FOR TODAY: We decree that Jesus is LORD! We will not fear what man can do to us!

Father, in Jesus' Name, we praise your Holy Name! Thank you for the power that is in the Name of Jesus! Our souls rejoice in you, Lord. We pray for those that don't feel like rejoicing, and those that are going through difficult situations. Some need added strength, Lord, because situations seem unbearable. But, we know that you are our source! You are our mind regulator! You are our hope when things seem hopeless! Glory to God! We pray for the renewing of minds today, Lord. We pray for those that seem overwhelmed because of the cares of this world. You have not given us the spirit of fear, but one of power, love and a sound mind. We rebuke the adversary. We speak peace in homes. We speak wellness in our bodies. We take authority over our atmosphere and we plead the blood of Jesus against everything that is not like you! We are victorious. We are winners. We are overcomers because of the power you have put within us. Help us to think it! To know it! God we thank you for living in us. In Jesus' Name, we give you the glory!

MAY 5

Psalm 48:14

For such is God, Our God forever and ever; He will guide us until death.

DECREE FOR TODAY: We decree that we are the children of the Most High, the lion of Judah, the Great I AM, and if we obey Him, nothing can stop what God has planned for us!

Father, in Jesus' Name, it is in you that we live, we move and have our being. Thank you! Without you, we are nothing. Without you, we couldn't breathe the air you have provided for our survival. God, help us not to take your provisions lightly. Thank you for the power of the Holy Ghost that lives within – causes us to maintain in the times of struggles and difficulties and times when we don't see our way! Thank you for understanding what the human part of us would need to survive the times, Lord. We give you glory! We honor your presence. We pray for those that are going through difficult mind situations. Lift up their bowed down heads, Lord. We pray they will be drawn into your presence where they will find joy and peace that surpasses all understanding. In Jesus' Name, we thank you Lord!

MAY 6

Psalm 119:50

This is my comfort in my affliction, That Your word has revived me.

DECREE FOR TODAY: We decree that we will not be intimidated this day but will answer every man with a soft answer, which turns away wrath!

Father, in Jesus' Name, we come with a heart of thanksgiving, a heart of repentance, and a heart of gratefulness for your lovingkindness towards us. Thank you for the gladness you put within us. A merry heart doeth good like a medicine, but a broken spirit drieth the bones. We praise you, Lord! We give you all the glory. Your love is unmeasurable! Thank for the gift of the blood of Jesus so that whosoever believeth in you should not perish. Thank you for casting all of our sins behind Thy back, as Isaiah so said, Lord. Your word declares that you preserve all them that love you! We love you, Lord! Surely, you have borne our griefs and carried our sorrows. Help us to let go and let God – to rest in you, Lord! For they that seek the Lord shall not want any good thing. In Jesus' Name, we thank you!

MAY 7

Ecclesiastes 3:1-8

There is an appointed time for everything. And there is a time for every event under heaven-- A time to give birth and a time to die; A time to plant and a time to uproot what is planted. A time to kill and a time to heal; A time to tear down and a time to build up.

DECREE FOR TODAY: We decree that we will cease from anger because he that is soon angry dealeth foolishly!

Father, in Jesus' Name, thank you for this miraculous gift of life. Hallelujah! We don't take it lightly that you shook us with your hand of grace, and woke us up in our right minds, with a desire to go forward, a desire to conquer, a desire to walk by faith and not by sight! Glory to God! In the midst of this corrupt world, Lord, you have given us the armour of God so that we can withstand in this evil day. We will use our shield of faith to quench all of the fiery darts thrown at us on the job, in the home, on the street, in church, or wherever we are! We are going to take advantage of this helmet of salvation and daily use the Word of God, which is our sword of the Spirit, to fight this good fight of faith, Lord. We won't use our mouths, our actions or our friends to fight for us because the battles belong to you, Lord. We are going to pray and pray and pray our way through here. We won't faint! We will be strong in you and in the power of your might! In Jesus' Name, we thank you!

MAY 8

Zephaniah 3:17

The LORD your God is in your midst, A victorious warrior He will exult over you with joy, He will be quiet in His love, He will rejoice over you with shouts of joy.

DECREEE FOR TODAY: We decree that we will let go and let God! God's got it!

Father, in Jesus' Name, thank you for the blood of Jesus that never loses its power. Thank you for the Name of Jesus that is all powerful. Your presence in us makes us powerful – gives us authority over the demonic forces of this world, gives us joy when it looks like it's over, and gives us peace in the midst of chaos and confusion. Glory to God! We appreciate the love. No greater love hath any man shown towards us than that which you have shown. Hallelujah! Our souls rejoice in the God of our salvation. Our minds are renewed daily. Our strength goes from strength to strength. When all else fails, we have this Hope that lies within us that causes us the rise above what we see! We walk by faith and not by sight. We are calling those things that are not as though they were! We see victory! We see healing! We see deliverance! We see provision! You said we could speak to our mountains! We are speaking life. We are speaking provision! We are speaking our way through here in the Name of Jesus we thank you Lord!

MAY 9

Ephesians 4:32

Be kind to one another, tender-hearted, forgiving each other, just as God in Christ also has forgiven you.

DECREE: We decree that the blood of Jesus is still as fresh today as it was at Calvary. It will work for us!

Father, in Jesus' Name, what a privilege it is to be chosen, to be identified with the King of the earth, to be called special people, a royal priesthood, and your chosen vessels to carry your Spirit on the inside. Glory to God! Thank you for calling us out of darkness into this marvelous light! Hallelujah! Thank you, Jesus, for your anointing that breaks every yoke. Thank you for giving us a mind to desire the things of you, Lord. Thank you for softening our hearts, and taking out our stony hearts. Help us to show the love of God towards one another. As we acknowledge you, direct our speech. Help us to respond in love but also with the authority that you have given us to walk on the devil's head. Oh, what power you have invested in us. Help us not to use this power to exalt ourselves but rather that your Name will be glorified in the earth! In Jesus' Name, we thank you Lord!

MAY 10

Psalm 100:5

For the LORD is good; His lovingkindness is everlasting And His faithfulness to all generations.

DECREE FOR TODAY: We decree that the righteous cry, the Lord hearth and delivereth them out of ALL of their troubles! God said so!

Father, in Jesus' Name, we bless your Name today. Great is thy faithfulness towards all men. You are the God of the Universe. All souls belongs to you. Thank you for the privilege to inherit eternal life. What a miracle you have given us! Thank you for the strength you give unto your people. You bless us with peace in the midst of storms. Glory to God! We give you thanks for making us partakers of the inheritance of the saints. Thank you for Favor! You see every sparrow that falls to the ground! You declared that even the hairs of our heads are numbered, fear thou not for we are of more value than many sparrows. We are confident that you will perform the good work you have begun in us till the day of Jesus Christ. In Jesus' Name, we thank you, Lord!

MAY 11

Ephesians 5:1-2

Therefore be imitators of God, as beloved children; and walk in love, just as Christ also loved you and gave Himself up for us, an offering and a sacrifice to God as a fragrant aroma.

DECREE FOR TODAY: We decree that victory is ours, on the job in the home, on the street, wherever! It is already done – whatever it is! We will look at things the way God sees them – already done!

Father, in the Name of Jesus we give you glory, we give you honor for your greatness. Hallelujah! Thank you for a brand new day. Thank you for life! Thank you for provision. Thank you for all things, for this is your will for your people and they are working together for our good. We come into your presence with a praise for whatever is going on because you are in control. You are, Lord! You own the world and all that is in it. Nothing is happening that you are not aware of, for this we give you glory! Every battle belongs to you! Every crooked place will be made straight. Every mountain will come down. We believe it, Lord! Some are trusting in flesh, but we will remember the Name of the Lord! We will be strong. We will endure hardness as good soldiers! We will allow your mind to be in our minds. We yield ourselves to you and receive the peace of God that surpasses all understanding. In Jesus' Name, we thank you!

MAY 12

<u>1 Corinthians 10:13</u>

No temptation has overtaken you but such as is common to man; and God is faithful, who will not allow you to be tempted beyond what you are able, but with the temptation will provide the way of escape also, so that you will be able to endure it.

DECREE FOR TODAY: We decree that we are blessed in the city, blessed in the field, wherever we are because of obedience! Tell the devil God said so and he can't stop it!

Father, in Jesus' Name, thank you for giving us a heart after you, Lord. Your word declares that it is with the heart man believeth unto righteousness. We won't allow our hearts to be troubled, Lord! We will rest in you! We know that heaviness in the heart of a man maketh it stoop, but a good word maketh it glad! That is your word! Bless you Lord – you daily load us with benefits. You are the God of our salvation. You are able to do exceeding abundantly above all that we ask or think according to the power that worketh in us! Thank you for the power of the Holy Ghost. We have this confidence in you that if we ask any thing according to your will, you hear us! And we know you hear us. We know we have the petitions that we desire of you! We are calling those things that are not as though they were. We will call on your Name until the high places come down, Glory to God! In Jesus' Name, we thank you!

MAY 13

Philippians 4:6

Be anxious for nothing, but in everything by prayer and supplication with thanksgiving let your requests be made known to God.

DECREE FOR TODAY: We decree that the God in us is greater than anything we will encounter this day!

Father, in Jesus' Name, thank you for the truth and for setting us free. Your word declares that we shall know the truth and the truth shall make us free. Thanks be unto God which always causes us to triumph in Christ. You are our strength, our shield. Our hearts trust in you. And for those that trust in you, Lord, you will do as you did for David - he said you delivered his soul in peace from the battle that was against him. Every battle has been fought for us! Thank you for being a warrior on behalf of your people. Thank you for supplying all of our needs according to your riches in glory by Christ Jesus. Thank you for the promise that the desire of the righteous shall be granted. We will not fear! We will not be dismayed! We won't be afraid of the terror by night nor the arrows that fly by day! When the enemy comes in like a flood, the Spirit of the Lord will lift up a standard against him. We thank you for healing the broken in heart and binding up their wounds. In Jesus' Name, we thank you Lord!

MAY 14

Psalm 42:11

Why are you in despair, O my soul? And why have you become disturbed within me? Hope in God!

DECREE FOR TODAY: We decree that we will go forth, fearing nothing! God said fear thou not!

Father, in Jesus' Name, thank you for your goodness, your mercy, and your longsuffering. You've been good to us, Lord. Hallelujah! You've delivered us from the powers of darkness, provided for us, healed us, and lifted us from pits that the enemy set up for us. Glory to God! Thank you, Jesus!

You've had patience with us when we have not been what we ought to be. You've delivered us and raised us to sit together in heavenly places. The things you have done for us are marvelous in our eyes. Forgive us, Lord, for not always remembering what you have done and failing to give you all the glory! Day after day, you watch over us. You have given us angels to assist us. You have kept our feet from being taken by the enemy. Glory to God. You have strengthened us when we were weak. Oh, Lord God, how can we ever forget your lovingkindness towards your people. Thank you for the blood-covering. Your blood will never lose its power. Help us to hide ourselves under the wings of the Almighty! Thank you Lord, in Jesus' Name!

MAY 15

Isaiah 26:3

The steadfast of mind You will keep in perfect peace, Because he trusts in You.

DECREE FOR TODAY: We decree that God is our ROCK! We will Stand, in spite of our situations and challenges! God's got us!

Father, in Jesus' Name, we say Hallelujah! We give you the highest praise. The Joy of the Lord is our strength. Thank you for the peace of God that you have given to your people. We pray for those that are feeling some kind of way today, Lord. We pray that they will be encouraged. None of us are always on the mountain, but you told us to comfort one another even as we are comforted. We pray for those going through difficult times, hard struggles, but we are encouraged by your word that says many are the afflictions of the righteous, but the Lord delivereth them out of them all! There will be victory after this! We speak life! We shall live and not die. The just SHALL live by faith! We pray for troubled hearts, you said let not your heart be troubled! You are our sustainer and our hope in hopeless situations. You speak and things happen! Your word has spoken and it shall not return void but it shall accomplish whereunto you have sent it. In the hospitals, in the homes, on the jobs, on the battle fields, wherever – your word will STAND! In Jesus' Name, we thank you!

MAY 16

Philippians 4:6-7

Be anxious for nothing, but in everything by prayer and supplication with thanksgiving let your requests be made known to God. And the peace of God, which surpasses all comprehension, will guard your hearts and your minds in Christ Jesus.

DECREE FOR TODAY: We decree that we will fear no man! God in us is greater than man and the enemy of our souls!

Father, in Jesus' Name, thank you for this good day! Every day that we wake up in the land of the living is a good day! No matter what takes place in it, Lord, your word says this is the day that the Lord has made. We will rejoice and be glad in it. Thank you for the gift of life, the gift of the Holy Ghost that keeps us, guides us, provides strength in times of weakness, and gives us boldness to stand against the wiles of the devil. Glory to God! We worship you today. We lift our hands in praise for who you are in our lives, in the earth and in the heavens. Thank you for the authority you have so freely given us to speak into our lives and call those things that are not as though they were. We are going to change our atmosphere by saying Hallelujah, Thank you God, Glory to your Name! Thank you Jesus for the power that is in your Name!

MAY 17

Jeremiah 32:27

Behold, I am the LORD, the God of all flesh; is anything too difficult for Me?

DECREE FOR TODAY: We decree that they that wait upon the LORD shall renew their strength; they shall mount up with wings as eagles; they shall run, and not be weary; and they shall walk, and not faint. Tell the devil the Word says so!

Father, in Jesus' Name, thank you for quickening us, delivering us from our sins and saving us by your grace! Glory to God! And thank you for raising us up together and making us to sit together in heavenly places in you Jesus! We honor you for your great gift of salvation through faith, Lord. Your grace, your unmerited favor towards us has saved us, delivered us from the hands of Satan. Oh, God, how we thank you today! And not only to us, but this gift is available to our children. Thank you, God! Save the unsaved children today that are willing to call on your Name. They need you in this wicked world, Lord. Help us to be sincere and without offense. We thank you Lord, in Jesus' Name!

MAY 18

John 8:32
You will know the truth, and the truth will make you free.

DECREE FOR TODAY: We decree that the Lord will give strength to his people. The Lord will bless his people with peace. He said so!

Father, in Jesus' Name, we are grateful to you for your lovingkindness, grateful for your patience, your long-suffering that allows your people to mature into a level of peace, rest and joy in the Holy Ghost. You've never left us nor forsaken us. Through it all, you've been our shelter, our comforter, and our deliverer from things we thought would capture us. Glory to God! Lord, we desire to please you; we desire that our faith level will rise above what our eyes see so that we can soar like the eagle does, above the storms of this life. Thank you for being mighty in battle, our strong tower, and our hiding place in the midst of a world that is falling apart. You remain the same. You keep our minds intact. You strengthen our hearts so that we are not overwhelmed, not fearful, and not doubtful, when we reach the faith level that you desire we achieve. Thank you for the Hope that lies within us. For every battle belongs to you and we need not fight in them, for we are more than conquerors if we stand still. In Jesus' Name, we thank you, Lord!

MAY 19

Nehemiah 8:10
Then he said to them, Go, eat of the fat, drink of the sweet, and send portions to him who has nothing prepared; for this day is holy to our Lord. Do not be grieved, for the joy of the LORD is your strength.

DECREE FOR TODAY: We decree that God has chosen us and made us special, a royal priesthood and he will make us the head and not the tail. Tell the devil it is so!

Father, in Jesus' Name, thank you for the power of praise! You promised us a garment of praise for the spirit of heaviness. There is a spirit of heaviness in the atmosphere, a spirit of discouragement is traveling the atmosphere, and a spirit of giving up is moving through the atmosphere, but God you have already equipped us to defeat these demons of darkness. Great is our God! Great is your faithfulness! Not one faileth! Not one time have you forsaken your people! You are our battle-axe. We will speak your word today to edify, to lift up, and to encourage! Glory to God! Your word will stand when all else fails. Hallelujah for the Word of God, in Jesus' Name!

MAY 20

Psalm 46:1-3

God is our refuge and strength, A very present help in trouble. Therefore we will not fear, though the earth should change And though the mountains slip into the heart of the sea; Though its waters roar and foam, Though the mountains quake at its swelling pride.

DECREE FOR TODAY: We decree that the Lord will shut the lion-like mouths that rise against us on the job, in the home, wherever! Tell the devil it is so!

Father, in Jesus' Name, thank you for allowing your glory to rest in your people. Thank you for favor, your mercy and grace that follow us daily. We bless you, Lord! You preserve the soul of the saints! Order our steps in your Word. You are not the author of confusion, but of peace. We declare peace in the minds of your people. You always cause us to triumph in Christ! Your word declares that those that hearken unto you shall dwell safely and SHALL BE QUIET FROM FEAR of evil. Thank you for the angel of the Lord that encampeth round about those that reverence you, Lord, and delivereth them. You have dealt to every man the measure of faith. Our faith will not stand in the wisdom of men, but in the power of God! Thank you, Lord, for assuring us that the Just shall live by faith – faith to believe without seeing. In Jesus' Name, we thank you Lord!

MAY 21

Philippians 4:13

I can do all things through Him who strengthens me.

DECREE FOR TODAY: We decree that the eye of the LORD is upon them that fear him, upon them that hope in his mercy; to deliver their soul from death, and to keep them alive in famine.

Father, in Jesus' Name, thank you for your unmerited favor of grace that lifted our eyelids this morning, both saved and unsaved. You didn't pick and choose who to wake up but you extended the same grace to those who love you and those who don't take a minute to serve you. You said, all souls belong to you and it is not your will that any of us should perish. We are expecting your return, Lord. Help us to be witnesses to our families as well as the unrelated, that time is running out. We are looking for that blessed Hope's return. You said you are coming in an hour when we think not. Help us to be ready, Lord. Help us to set our houses in order, to be filled with your Spirit, to have the right attitudes, and to be conscious of our behavior not only around the saved but the unsaved. Help us to be real, Lord. You are not accepting anything less. Take us through this day, Lord, knowing that all things, no matter how rough, are working for our good. Glory to God and we thank you, in Jesus' Name!

MAY 22

Psalm 34:4

I sought the LORD, and He answered me, And delivered me from all my fears.

DECREE FOR TODAY: We decree that the LORD will bless the righteous; with favour will the Lord compass him as with a shield. Tell the demons God said so!

Father, in Jesus' Name, thank you for the power of prayer. Thank you for the power of praise. Oh, Glory to your Name! God, if we could only take hold of prayer, it is a tool that will bring down strongholds, change conditions in the world, and bring peace in our homes and on our jobs! It will change lives! Oh, God, the garment of praise will replace the spirit of heaviness. Thank you, God! We praise you for victory today. We say Glory! We say Hallelujah! We say the joy of the Lord is our strength! Oh yes, Satan, God has given us weapons against your armies. Nothing can harm us. We are spirit-minded. We give our minds over to God and no weapon formed against us shall prosper. Thank you, Lord, for the mind to think and to be able to use our minds as sifters to sift out every thought that would hinder us. In Jesus' Name, we thank you!

MAY 23

<u>Matthew 11:30</u>

All things have been handed over to Me by My Father; and no one knows the Son except the Father; nor does anyone know the Father except the Son, and anyone to whom the Son wills to reveal Him.

DECREE FOR TODAY: We decree that the devil had nothing to do with creating this day- we won't give him any space! For this is the day that the Lord has made. We will rejoice and be glad in it.

Father, in Jesus' Name, we thank you for the opportunity to be able to call upon you at any given moment, day or night and you hear us. Your ears are open to the cries of your people. We are grateful for your love, God. It is unmeasurable! You never fail us. You never make us feel unworthy of your grace and mercy even though we don't deserve it. Glory to God! We thank you that we don't have to worry about the tactics of the devil. You see his mind. You see his plans. You see what he has given to the demons of hell to carry out against your people. Thank you for interceding. Oh, how you protect us from the unknown. We give you glory. We honor you, Lord. Help us not to forget to say thank you for all that you do for us, in Jesus' Name!

MAY 24

<u>1 Thessalonians 4:13</u>

But we do not want you to be uninformed, brethren, about those who are asleep, so that you will not grieve as do the rest who have no hope.

DECREE FOR STAY: We decree that we will ride out our storms! Every Christian has a storm. But the God that lives in us is greater than our storms! Yes He is!

Father, in Jesus' Name, thank you for the Word of God! Oh, how precious is this word. God help us to hide it in our hearts for there is coming a famine in the land, not for food, not for water, but the hearing of the Word of God! Help us to store it up in us so that when the enemy arrives, we can defeat him with the Word of God, not weapons, not swords of words or actions but simply with the Word of God! Help us to put the Word of God in our children so that they will know the power of the Word in their lives. Bless us so that we will take time to read your word, to pray, and to talk to you. You are ready to talk; help us to listen, Lord! We thank you for lifting the bowed down heads today, the crushed in spirit, and the lowly for you are our God, the great I AM! Thank you God, in Jesus' Name!

MAY 25

Isaiah 49:13

Shout for joy, O heavens! And rejoice, O earth! Break forth into joyful shouting, O mountains! For the LORD has comforted His people And will have compassion on His afflicted.

DECREE FOR TODAY: We decree that if God be for us, He is more than the world against us! Tell devil it is so!

Father, in Jesus' Name, we rest in you, Lord! We trust in your Word! Thank you for leaving your Word and your Spirit in the earth. We give you glory and praise for making us victorious in every situation. Things we don't see, you divinely make them known to us. Things we don't understand, we lean to you. Your ways are not like our ways. Your thoughts are not like our thoughts. Thank you for putting a praise in us that allows us to give you some glory in the midst of whatever we are going through. You've made the crooked places straight. You have already answered every prayer. Help us to recognize that the answers are in place and we need only to wait patiently for you, Lord! Thank you for the power that is in the Name of Jesus! For you are greater in us than the evil forces in the world. Thank you that these battles belong to you and not us, Lord! We rest in you, Lord, in Jesus' Name!

MAY 26

1 John 4:7

Beloved, let us love one another, for love is from God; and everyone who loves is born of God and knows God.

DECREE FOR TODAY: We decree that we won't allow the enemy to take our joy! God gave it to us and the devil can't take it away unless we allow him to do it! We won't! God in us is bigger than that!

Father, in Jesus' Name, we come boldly before you and yet humbly, acknowledging your greatness in the earth and in our lives! Hallelujah! We press in, Lord, seeking a closer relationship with you. You are our hiding place from the chaos in the world. Glory to God! We appreciate your listening ear, your faithfulness to us, your forgiveness and forgetfulness of our sins. Thank you, Lord! We have this treasure within us that allows us to soar when we don't feel like it. It allows us to go forward when we don't see our way! It allows us to speak with authority that causes the atmosphere around us to be pleasant, even in the midst of confusion, doubt and things that just don't look good. We say Glory to God in the highest that causes our minds to leap over situations that seem to try to block our thinking! In Jesus' Name, we thank you Lord!

MAY 27

Matthew 11:28-30

Come to Me, all who are weary and heavy-laden, and I will give you rest. "Take My yoke upon you and learn from Me, for I am gentle and humble in heart, and YOU WILL FIND REST FOR YOUR SOULS." For My yoke is easy and My burden is light.

DECREE FOR TODAY: We decree that we will seek to daily tell God thank you; whatever is going on, tell God thank you!

Father, in Jesus' thank you, Lord, for your rich mercy and your great love. Thank you for raising us up together and allowing us to sit together in heavenly places in Christ Jesus. Thank you for preserving us, Lord. You promised that if we abide in you and your word abide in us, we shall ask what we will and it shall be done unto us – according to your divine will! It is your will that we will prosper and be in health, even as our soul prospers. We come boldly to your throne asking for comfort for those that are feeling down, Lord. We pray for strength for those that are weary. You are our strength, our strong tower. No weapon formed against us shall prosper, regardless of its form! We have been sanctified, we have been justified, and we have been armed with your power to defeat every adversary we encounter. Glory to God! We declare victory over demons, over ourselves, over people, over attitudes and whatever comes against us. In Jesus' Name, we thank you Lord!

MAY 28

<u>Isaiah 55:8</u>

For My thoughts are not your thoughts, Nor are your ways My ways, declares the LORD.

DECREE FOR TODAY: We decree that if we seek first the kingdom of God and his righteousness, everything we need will be added unto us! Tell the devil God said so!

Father, in Jesus' Name, you have kept us through the night, through the day, through trials and tribulations, hardships, disappointments, failures and so much more, but we are still here. Glory to God! We feel your presence in the earth at a level of anointing that we have not experienced before, Lord. You are getting your people ready for great things to come! Hallelujah! The world may be in chaos, but we can feel that you are getting ready to move by your power in the earth! God we pray for those children that are being neglected and abused. We pray for their deliverance. We pray for women and men involved in domestic violence. We speak peace in that home right NOW, in the Name of Jesus. Thank you for your peace Lord, in Jesus' Name!

MAY 29

<u>Isaiah 55:9</u>

For as the heavens are higher than the earth, So are My ways higher than your ways And My thoughts than your thoughts.

DECREE FOR TODAY: We decree that we will NOT render evil for evil! The battle is not ours. It belongs to the Lord!

Father, in Jesus' Name, thank you that we can cleave unto you, our God! We will stand fast in the liberty wherein you have set us free, Lord. We won't be entangled again with the yoke of bondage! Thank you for the Holy Ghost that is available to enable us to do so! We will be steadfast, unmovable and abound in the work you have given us Lord. You promised that the righteous shall hold on his way. We won't be weary in well doing for in due season you have promised that we shall reap if we faint not! We will hope to the end, Lord! We won't be carried away with strange doctrines. We will let our hearts be established with grace, holding on and asking in faith, not wavering but believing that what you have promised you are able to perform. We thank you for it, Lord, in Jesus' Name!

MAY 30

<u>Psalm 92:5</u>
How great are Your works, O LORD! Your thoughts are very deep.

DECREE FOR TODAY: We decree that we will not be bound by anything nor anybody. The Blood of Jesus has set us free! Walk in freedom in the mind and spirit! It belongs to us! People can only do to us what we allow them to do! We are free! Tell the devil it is so!

Father, in Jesus' Name, thank you! We thank you for being the great I AM, the Almighty, Prince of Peace, our Counselor, our Healer, our Deliverer, our Blessed Hope! You are all that we need Lord. We will continue to look to you, for in you we are complete! No good thing will you withhold from those that walk uprightly. You are our shield and buckler, our defense in the time of trouble. There is none like you, Lord! We stretch out in faith, knowing that it is impossible to please you without it. All of your promises are yea and amen! Every struggle, every battle, and everything that touches our lives have already been worked out by you. We need only to wait for things to be manifested. Your word says, we are more than conquerors! Thank you for the blood of Jesus that covers us! In Jesus' Name!

MAY 31

<u>Amos 4:13</u>
For behold, He who forms mountains and creates the wind And declares to man what are His thoughts, He who makes dawn into darkness And treads on the high places of the earth, The LORD God of hosts is His name.

DECREE FOR TODAY: We decree that it is well! Regardless of the situation, it is well!

Father, in Jesus' Name, thank you for this opportunity to talk to you, Lord. We don't take it lightly. Your goodness towards us is unmeasurable! Oh how great is your goodness that is laid up for all that reverence you. We would have fainted unless we had seen your goodness in the land of the living, in the midst of chaos. Thank you for being our refuge and strength, upholding us when we couldn't see our way, and directing us when we don't see what's waiting. God, we thank you! You have promised to sustain us, if we cast our cares upon you. We pray for deliverance for those that are bound in the mind, bound by drugs, and bound by alcohol. Set them free, Lord, from the powers that hold them hostage. Continue to use our mouths to spread the gospel of peace, love and joy that is full of glory. Mend marriages. Heal broken and wounded spirits, Lord. Thank you, in Jesus' Name!

JUNE 1

Micah 4:12

But they do not know the thoughts of the LORD, And they do not understand His purpose; For He has gathered them like sheaves to the threshing floor.

DECREE FOR TODAY: We decree that we will yield our tongues to the Spirit so that we can give a soft answer, for it turneth away wrath!

Father, in Jesus' Name, we approach your throne in boldness and yet in humbleness, acknowledging your greatness in us and in the earth! Hallelujah! There is no condemnation to them that are in Christ Jesus. Thank you for forgiveness of our sins - those we committed and those we thought about. Your grace and mercy are unexplainable! We glory in your presence, Lord. God, we thank you for the use of our limbs. We can't do anything without you, but thank God we can do all things through Christ that strengthens us. Your word declares that these signs shall follow them that believe – in your Name we shall cast out devils. We rebuke every demon that is attacking your people's minds, the homes, and the jobs. We command them to come out of the atmosphere, get out of our space, in the Name of Jesus. Thank you for the power of the Holy Ghost, in Jesus' Name!

JUNE 2

Psalm 40:5

Many, O LORD my God, are the wonders which You have done, And Your thoughts toward us; There is none to compare with You If I would declare and speak of them, They would be too numerous to count.

DECREE FOR TODAY: We decree that we will not fear man, what man says, what man puts in place, what man tries to take away from us! For our God is a Spirit and the Spirit in us is greater than flesh of man!

Father, in Jesus' Name, great is thy mercy towards us. Your compassions fail not! Hallelujah! Today, Lord, we come boldly to your throne with your permission to ask anything according to your will and you will do it. Heal sick bodies, Lord. Many are in pain. We rebuke the pain at the root. Raise up those that need strength in their bodies. Renew minds. We rebuke the attack of the enemy on the minds of your people. We speak peace. We speak deliverance. We speak victory, for your word declares we are more than conquerors through Christ Jesus. Help us to focus on you and not the cares of this world. Help us not to be consumed with daily happenings so much so that we forget the power of prayer, the power of fasting and reading your word! Your Word is our sword. Help us to remind ourselves that we are walking around with the God of the Universe on the inside and there is no fear in you. God we thank you for it today, in Jesus' Name!

JUNE 3

<u>Psalm 139:17</u>

How precious also are Your thoughts to me, O God! How vast is the sum of them!

DECREE: We decree that we will not be intimidated by the news, people, nor anything that rises up against us! Greater is He that is in us than he that is in the world. Tell the devil God said so!

Father, in Jesus' Name, we are determined to wait upon you. We will be strong and let our hearts take courage. Your word declares that you are good to those that wait for you. Our hope is in your word! We have no doubts that you have begun a good work in us and you will complete it until the day of Christ when you rapture us and take us to glory, Lord! We know that in quietness and confidence is our strength. We will lie down and sleep in peace for it is you, Lord, that causes us to dwell in safety. We will not be afraid of sudden fear! We will not be shaken for you are our Rock! Our fortress! Our deliverer! Our shelter in a time of a storm! We will remain rooted in you, building ourselves up praying in the Holy Ghost. We take authority over everything that is not like you, Lord, pulling down strongholds and casting down every imagination that exalts itself against you! We thank you for the power, in Jesus' Name!

JUNE 4

Psalm 46:10

Be still, and know that I am God. I will be exalted among the nations, I will be exalted in the earth!

DECREE FOR TODAY: We decree that the joy that we have, the world didn't give it to us and the world can't take it away! The joy of the Lord is our strength!

Father, in Jesus' Name, thank you for strengthening us with all power according to your might, Lord, so that we can have endurance, joy and patience! We won't grow weary, for in due season you have promised that we will reap if we faint not. Your word says happy is the man that endures trials, for when we have stood our tests, Lord, we will receive the crown of life that is promised to all of us that endure to the end. Glory to God! We know the race is not given to the swift nor the battle to the strong. You make us stand strong. You are great and greatly to be praised! You do great wonders and you are King of the earth! We rest in you, Lord, knowing that you are in control of all things and according to this power that you have put in us and works in us, you are able to do far more abundantly beyond all that we ask or even think! Thank you Lord, in Jesus' Name!

JUNE 5

Psalm 119:89

For ever, O LORD, thy word is settled in heaven.

DECREE FOR TODAY: We decree that we will not worry about the unknown! We serve the God that knows and controls the unknown! Tell the devil it is so!

Father, in Jesus' Name, we bless you for your kindness, your goodness and your faithfulness to us. We give you thanks in all circumstances for we know that whatever state we are in, we will overcome every obstacle. You said, many are the afflictions of the righteous, but the Lord delivereth them out of them all! We won't be anxious. It is you that have made us and we are the sheep of your pasture. It is in you that we live, we move, and we have our being! Glory to God! Help us to express your love. We won't be rude and easily angered. We won't keep record of others wrong doings to us, but we will forgive and forget even as you have forgiven us, Lord! We won't hate, as it stirs up dissension. We will put on love for it binds us together in perfect unity on the job, in the home, and wherever we are because your word says whoever does not love, does not know you. For you are love. God, we thank you, in Jesus' Name!

JUNE 6

<u>Psalm 34:8</u>

O taste and see that the LORD is good: blessed is the man that trusteth in him.

DECREE FOR TODAY: We decree that our hope is in God! His track record indicates not one faileth!

Father, in Jesus' Name, thank you for being a God full of compassion, and gracious, longsuffering and plenteous in mercy and truth. You are King over the entire earth! You sit upon the throne of your holiness and your eyes run to and fro in the earth beholding the good and the evil. Lord, you know the days of the upright, and you promised they will not be ashamed in the evil time and in the days of famine, they shall be satisfied! Hallelujah! How excellent is your lovingkindness, Lord! With you is the fountain of life and in thy light we shall we see light. Thank you for favor! Thank you for making us the head and not the tail. Your blessings will overtake us - run us down if we obey your word! Thank you for considering our troubles and knowing our adversities. For you are our hiding place. We thank you for it, in Jesus' Name!

JUNE 7

<u>1 Corinthians 13:13</u>

So now faith, hope, and love abide, these three; but the greatest of these is love.

DECREE FOR TODAY: We decree that we will walk in love, as Christ hath loved us! Nothing will separate us from the love of Christ

– on the job, in the home, in the church, on the street, wherever! Tell the devil it is so!

Father, in Jesus' Name, we honor your presence, your Name, and your authority in our lives and in the earth. Oh, what a privilege it is to be allowed to carry your Spirit within us! Hallelujah! What a privilege to be able to use your Name, the Name of Jesus, which has all power in earth and in heaven! What armor you have equipped us with to fight the good fight of faith so that we can finish our course and lay hold onto eternal life! Glory to God! Strengthen the weak in spirit. Continue to heal sick bodies. Your faithfulness to us and in this earth has kept the body of Christ afloat in a chaotic world. Thank you, God! We appreciate your mercy and your forgiveness when we have failed to obey you or failed to trust you. Your longsuffering is unmatchable! We will lift our banners of praise in the midst of hardships and sorrows for you have given us the garment of praise for the spirit of heaviness. Thank you Lord, in Jesus' Name!

JUNE 8

John 3:16

For God so loved the world that he gave his one and only Son, that whoever believes in him shall not perish but have eternal life.

DECREE FOR TODAY: We decree that we will abide in the Lord, therefore we can ask him anything according to his will and it shall be done! Tell the devil it is so!

Father, in Jesus' Name, thank you for the power of God that dwells within us that keeps us from so easily being removed from this great gospel! We won't quench the spirit. We give you full reign in our lives, Lord, as our King, our Lord, our battle axe, our healer and deliverer and all that we need! Victory is our Name. We won't give space to the enemies of our soul and minds. Thank you for not allowing the sun to overheat and scorch us in this period of Grace! Lord, we thank you that you did not give man control of the air we breathe otherwise we would be robbed, overcharged and some even cut off. Glory to God! We bless you for controlling the things that come against your people. Every step we take will be one of faith, looking the impossibilities in the face, looking the painful trials in the face and believing that what you have promised MUST come to past. You are not a man; you don't tell lies. God we thank you, in Jesus' Name!

JUNE 9

Jeremiah 32:27
Behold, I am the LORD, the God of all flesh; is anything too difficult for Me?

DECREE FOR TODAY: We decree that the just SHALL live by faith. Every high place must come down! Tell the devil it is so!

Father, in Jesus' Name, thank you for the Cross. Thank you for shedding your blood for us. Thank you for loving us enough to dwell inside of us for we cannot come to you unless you draw us! Hallelujah! We praise you for taking away all of our sins, renewing us, and giving us hope in a hopeless world that seems to be beyond what you intended it to be. God, we thank you for perseverance, for putting a drive in us to press on toward the mark of the high calling of God in Christ Jesus. Through all of our trials, our tests, our heartaches, disappointments, sickness and failures, you have been there. You have raised your people up to sit together in high places in Christ Jesus. You have given us the power to overcome every obstacle. The Blood still works! Oh, God, thank you that the Blood still works! Help us to stay under the blood of Jesus, for in you, Lord, is safety for your people. We thank you for it, in Jesus' Name!

JUNE 10

Isaiah 50:10
Who is among you that fears the LORD, That obeys the voice of His servant, That walks in darkness and has no light? Let him trust in the name of the LORD and rely on his God.

DECREE FOR TODAY: We decree that every chain is broken, every stronghold is brought down in the Name of Jesus! We are free!

Father, in Jesus' Name, thank you for this great gift of prayer. You said we can ask you anything in your Name according to your divine will and you will do it. We believe it, Lord! We are stretching out in our faith today, calling those things that are not as though they were. We claim our healing in the Name of Jesus. Whatever way you choose to do it, we accept it as your will. We claim provision. We claim the peace that is already guaranteed if we keep our minds stayed on you. We claim salvation for our children as it is promised to us and our children. We take you at your word, Lord. The world is going to and fro, but we will be still and see the salvation of the Lord! We will wait patiently for you, Lord. We won't be moved! In Jesus' Name, we thank you Lord!

JUNE 11

Philippians 1:21
For to me to live is Christ, and to die is gain.

DECREE FOR TODAY: We decree that we will call those things that are not as though they were! We will speak it for the power of life and death is in our tongues!

Father, in Jesus' Name, thank you for bringing us through our tests. Your mercy covered all of us. Many went through difficult times, many are still going through some pain, and many are rejoicing through it all. For you have not forsaken your people. You presence goes with us. Hallelujah! Thank you for saving us. Renewing us! Lifting us and giving us strength to go forward. Thank you for the use of our limbs. We praise you for our eyes and to be able to read your encouragements. Thank you for establishing us in the faith, rooting us and grounding us in love for one another. We pray for broken homes, broken-hearted, even broken-hearted children that you will draw them to you and that they will seek your face for mending. You are our Joy! Our hope! Our healer! Everything we need is in you and we thank you for it in Jesus' Name!

JUNE 12

Matthew 7:7
Ask, and it shall be given you; seek, and ye shall find; knock, and it shall be opened unto you!

DECREE FOR TODAY: We decree that nothing shall separate us from the love of God. No demon, no friend, no family member, no enemy, nobody shall have power over us! Tell that to the devil!

Father, in Jesus' Name, thank you for making the thoughts of the righteous right and for the casting down of imaginations and every high thing that exalteth itself against the knowledge of you, Lord. Continue to help us that our mouths will bring forth wisdom, knowing that our old man is crucified with you, Lord, that the body of sin might be destroyed. We will keep our hearts with all diligence. For with our hearts, we believe unto righteousness, expecting that inheritance incorruptible and undefiled and that fadeth not away, which you have reserved for us in heaven. Glory to God. We thank you Lord, in Jesus' Name!

JUNE 13

Psalm 16:8

I have set the LORD always before me: because he is at my right hand, I shall not be moved.

DECREE FOR TODAY: We decree that we will not try to handle things. We will allow the God inside of us to go before us! He will bring down every stronghold! He will make the crooked straight! Tell the devil God said so!

Father, in Jesus' Name, thank you for allowing us to open our eyes and wake up to a new day; and whatever it holds, Lord, we say thank you! Praise you for the strength, the endurance, and the Holy Ghost that directs our steps day after day. Thank you for the miracle of life. You didn't allow the enemy to take us out. Many times, we fell short but your mercy and grace are still following us day by day. Hallelujah! Great is your faithfulness. Your compassions are new every morning! We pray for those with heavy hearts, and those that seem to be overwhelmed with the cares of this world. We pray that they will cast them upon you, Lord. Some are saying, that's not easy to do. Take over their minds, Lord, and help them to not only believe but to know that you will never leave us nor forsake us and that through every battle, every trial, and every dark place that you are there and deliverance is a promise. In Jesus' Name, we thank you!

JUNE 14

Isaiah 55:12

For ye shall go out with joy, and be led forth with peace: the mountains and the hills shall break forth before you into singing, and all the trees of the field shall clap their hands.

DECREE FOR TODAY: We decree that humans are only dust! We will not fear a single one of them.

Father, in Jesus' Name, oh to be close to you is our desire. Thank you for giving us admission to your glory and your presence Lord. Let the spirit of prayer fall upon your people. Help us not to just utter words but that we will press in until your Spirit takes over our prayers and makes intercession for us, for we know not what to pray for. Help us to tap into the faith you have given us, Lord, so that we will without doubt know that what you have promised will come to pass. Through faith they crossed the Red Sea, through faith kingdoms were subdued, and through faith lions mouths were shut. Help us, Lord, that as we hear your word, we will put it into action, for faith cometh by hearing and hearing by the word! Bless us to speak a word of life into someone today as we all go about our daily duties. Thank you Lord, in Jesus' Name!

JUNE 15

Matthew 6:33

But seek ye first the kingdom of God, and His righteousness; and all these things shall be added unto you.

DECREE FOR TODAY: We decree that victory belongs to us. We claim it on the job, in the home, wherever! God has already given it to us!

Father, in Jesus' Name, thank you for this moment in time and regardless of our locations, positions, circumstances, we are still here! Hallelujah! Lord, some of your people are experiencing difficult times in this life, some are angry, disappointed, fearful and just don't know what to do. But God help us to remember that you have a plan for our lives and nothing nor anyone can change it, if we walk upright before you. Your plans are not like our plans. Your thoughts are not like our thoughts. Help us to fear not! Your eyes run to and fro in the earth beholding the good and the evil! You are our strength. You are our Rock! You are our provider. Glory to God! You hold the world in the palm of your hands. We trust in you Lord our

Blessed hope for hope deferred maketh the heart sick. Thank you for hearing us when we call in Jesus' Name!

JUNE 16

<u>Psalms 89:1 I</u>

I will sing of the mercies of the LORD for ever: with my mouth will I make known thy faithfulness to all generations.

DECREE FOR TODAY: We decree that God has already delivered us in peace from every battle that comes against us! Tell the devil God said so!

Father, in the Name of Jesus thank you for the anointing that breaks the yokes. We are grateful for this power that works within us that gives us peace, joy, healing, deliverance and victory, day after day without fail! Hallelujah! Forgive us of our sins, wherever we have come short of your word, Lord. Thank you for daily renewing the strength of your people. We won't take down, Lord. We won't go back. We will go forward. We will endure hardness as good soldiers. We will speak with a soft answer but with confidence knowing that you are our source! We will not fear man nor anything that we encounter for you have already defeated the spirit of fear. Bless the children, Lord. We rebuke the bullies. Disarm them of that spirit that comes against our children, Lord. We speak peace over our children. In Jesus' Name, we thank you!

JUNE 17

<u>Psalm 46:10</u>

Be still, and know that I am God. I will be exalted among the nations, I will be exalted in the earth!

DECREE FOR TODAY: We degree that no demon can touch us without God's permission. And if God be for us, WHO can be against us!

Father, in Jesus' Name, thank you for being full of compassion and gracious, longsuffering and plenteous in mercy and truth. Incline your ear unto our cries, Lord. Give strength to your people. Many are afflicted by something, but you have promised to deliver them out of them all! Glory to

God! Praise you for giving us your anointing. Thank you for this power to bring down strongholds, to heal and deliver, even the minds of your people, Lord. We come against weariness! We speak peace. You said let not your heart be troubled. Troubled hearts are in the land, Lord. You have made us overcomers in every area. Help us to use faith to go forward regardless of the obstacles. Nothing is too hard for you! When you speak, the earth and everything in it has to listen. On the job, in the home, on the street, wherever, your Blood still works. In Jesus' Name, we thank you!

JUNE 18

Psalm 119:89

For ever, O LORD, thy word is settled in heaven.

DECREE FOR TODAY: We decree that no good thing will God withhold from them that walk upright!

Father, in Jesus' Name, thank you for prayer. Thank you for putting it into our minds that we have the ability to talk to the God of the Universe. Hallelujah! We can talk to you, Lord, about anything. Glory to God. What a privilege. We know you hear us. Your word declares it to be so. Bless those that are waiting for answers, Lord. You have not forgotten! Yea, you will not forget. Thank you for the power to call those things that are not as though they were. Thank you for establishing us, settling us in your Word. Your Word is like a hammer that breaketh the rock in pieces. We will use it to speak life into our dead situations; we will use it to speak healing, deliverance, and mending of broken relationships. Glory to God! You said better is the ending of a thing than the beginning. We wait patiently for you, Lord, enduring hardness as good soldiers in a chaotic world. In Jesus' Name, we thank you!

JUNE 19

1 Corinthians 13:13

So now faith, hope, and love abide, these three; but the greatest of these is love.

DECREE FOR TODAY: We decree that we will reject the intimidating demonic forces trying to discourage us! We have the power over them! God said so!

Father, in Jesus' Name, we praise you for creating us, giving us an opportunity to experience your glory, your anointing, the beauty of your creation. Lord, man has corrupted your creation, but in the midst of it, you keep your people. We appreciate your promise that no weapon formed against us shall prosper. You will be a refuge for the oppressed and a refuge in times of trouble. We are going to take the shield of faith so that we can quench all of the fiery darts of the enemy. We trust you, Lord, with all of our hearts. We won't lean unto our own understanding. Trusting in you, Lord, brings everlasting strength! Trusting in you, Lord, will keep us in perfect peace! Glory to God! We will hold fast our profession of our faith, without wavering, for you are faithful to your promises. In Jesus' Name, we thank you!

JUNE 20

John 3:16

For God so loved the world that he gave his one and only Son, that whoever believes in him shall not perish but have eternal life.

DECREE FOR TODAY: We decree that He that hath begun a good work in us will complete it until the day of Jesus Christ! Tell the devil God said so!

Father, in Jesus' Name, thank you for strength, thank you for a voice to say Hallelujah, thank you for the eyes you have given us to behold your beautiful creation. God we give you all the glory for this precious gift of the Holy Ghost that has armed us for the warfare of this life. Thank you for preparing us to endure hardness as good soldiers. We bless you for directing our steps so that we don't go down the road of destruction. Glory to God! We lift your Name today for it is a strong tower and the righteous runneth into it and is safe. Though we pass through the waters, you are with us, and through the rivers those difficult situations that seem like they will drown us, you don't allow them to overflow us, and when we walk through the fire, those moments when we feel like we will be completely destroyed by situations, by others or by the enemy, you won't let us be burned. God, we thank you for mercy and grace that follows us daily. This day, Lord we say Hallelujah! We say Glory! We say thank you Lord, in Jesus' Name!

JUNE 21

Jeremiah 32:27

Behold, I am the LORD, the God of all flesh; is anything too difficult for Me?

DECREE FOR TODAY: We decree that we will not be intimidated by anyone on the job, in the home, on the street, wherever! Haven't we heard, GREATER is he that is inside of us than he – the devil – that is in the world! God said so!

Father, in Jesus' Name, thank you for being Lord over our storms. When you speak, there is peace! Glory to God! We enter into your presence with thanksgiving and into your courts with praise! We don't take your goodness for granted. We appreciate your thoughts toward us, Lord, which are good and not evil and to give us an expected end. Thank you for taking over our spirits and not allowing the demons of hell to control us. Glory to God! Hallelujah, for this great power that is within us! We rejoice in the God of our salvation. We look forward to spending eternity with you, Lord. The days are short and evil, but we have this blessed hope within us that you have prepared a place for us where there will be no more dying, no more crying, and no more pain; oh Glory to our God! We will rest in you and do good, Lord. We will walk in our victory knowing that the blood of Jesus is covering us and our children! We thank you for it, Lord in Jesus' Name!

JUNE 22

Isaiah 50:10

Who is among you that fears the LORD, That obeys the voice of His servant, That walks in darkness and has no light? Let him trust in the name of the LORD and rely on his God.

DECREE FOR TODAY: We decree that we will rule our spirits and not be entangled with the influences of the devil! For he that ruleth his spirit is better than he that taketh a city! Tell the devil God's word says so!

Father, in Jesus' Name, thank you for your greatness. You are greatly to be praised. We give you the glory that is due your Name, Lord! We exalt you. Thank you for bringing us to this day. Help us to cherish each moment and make good use of the time you have given us. Lord, we pray that you will strengthen us with might by your Spirit in our inner man. Help us to stay rooted and grounded in love. Help us to know your love, Lord, that passeth knowledge so that we can be filled with all the fullness of God! Help us to redeem the time for the days are evil. We submit ourselves to you, to be used by you for your glory in the home, on the job, or wherever we are. We will not fear anything! Thank you for empowering us to conquer, to overcome, to excel, and to go forward knowing that all things are working together for our good. In Jesus' Name, we thank you!

JUNE 23

Philippians 1:21
For to me to live is Christ, and to die is gain.

DECREE FOR TODAY: We decree that we all of God's promises are yea and amen! We will wait for the promise!

Father, in Jesus' Name, thank you for giving us the gift of the Holy Ghost that equips us to live a stress-free life! Glory to God! We love you, Lord. We pray that we will all continue to keep our minds stayed on you. Lord, if we do that, you have promised to keep us in perfect peace. Hallelujah! Help us to wear this world as a loose garment and not become attached to it, Lord, because we brought nothing into it and we shall carry nothing with us when we depart. We rebuke the spirit of fear, weariness, tiredness and whatever spirits are attacking the body of Christ. We have the authority to cast them out of our space! Thank you, God! We give you glory for the power that is available to us to face every challenge knowing that the power within us gives us victory. In Jesus' Name, we thank you!

JUNE 24

Matthew 7:7
Ask, and it shall be given you; seek, and ye shall find; knock, and it shall be opened unto you: For every one that asketh receiveth; and he that seeketh findeth; and to him that knocketh it shall be opened.

DECREE FOR TODAY: We decree that just as David slew Goliath by facing him in the Name of the Lord, we will overcome every giant-like obstacle we face today by using the Name of Jesus! It is the most powerful Name in the earth! The devil knows it!

Father, in Jesus' we bless you today! Thank you for keeping us as we slept. Glory to God! Electrical wires running through our homes, but God you kept us! Hallelujah! We will walk in victory today, knowing that our King is in control. Regardless of our situations, you know how to handle them and strengthen us to move on. We wait on you, Lord. We will be still and let you be God. We are looking to the hills from whence cometh our help, for our help comes from the Lord! Thank you for not treating us according to our ways when we didn't obey you, Lord. Thank you for faith that can conqueror anything! Thank you for the joy of the Lord which is our strength. Thank you for trials for they come to make us. Thank you for the peace of God that surpasses all understanding. Help us to hold onto that. Bless your people today, Lord. In Jesus' Name, we thank you!

JUNE 25

<u>Psalm 16:8</u>

I have set the LORD always before me: because he is at my right hand, I shall not be moved.

DECREE FOR TODAY: Do you not know that demons have assigned territories (Daniel 10:13). Say it - I decree that this day the demon assigned to the atmosphere where I will be is defeated by the anointing of God that is present in my life. It is so in Jesus' Name!

Father, in Jesus' Name, we humble ourselves before you and give you thanks for all things. You have declared in your word that they are working for our good! Thank you for the word of God. It is food to our souls, a light unto our paths. Thank you for ordering our steps and watching over us as your eyes run to and fro in the earth beholding the good and the evil. We bless you, Lord. Nothing can separate us from you, neither life nor death, nor angels, nor height nor depth nor any other creature shall be able to separate us from your love! Having done all, we will stand! You promised to give strength to the weary and increase the power of the weak. We will use our faith to see beyond our now! For all of your promises are yea and amen! Oh Lord, we thank you, in Jesus' Name!

JUNE 26

Isaiah 55:12

For ye shall go out with joy, and be led forth with peace: the mountains and the hills shall break forth before you into singing, and all the trees of the field shall clap their hands.

DECREE FOR TODAY: We decree that by faith we will cross over our Red Seas today! Without fail, God will deliver us!

Father, in Jesus Name, thank you for caring for and loving us. Thank you that you always give us your undivided attention. You have millions of children in the earth that cry unto you day and night, and yet you make time to hear each of us. You are an amazing God! You are the only God; there is none else! Thank you for healing our bodies. Thank you for your provisions. Thank you for making plans for us before the foundation of the world! Glory to God! Thank you that each of us mean the world to you. You placed us in the earth for your glory! You perfectly designed each of us to fit and play a role in your kingdom; and you gave each of us a choice to accept it or refuse it. We are grateful for your love, Lord. We can't explain it, but we are grateful. Thank you for giving us angels to protect us. We bless your Name, Lord. You are a wonder in the earth. In Jesus' Name, we thank you!

JUNE 27

Matthew 6:33

But seek ye first the kingdom of God, and His righteousness; and all these things shall be added unto you.

DECREE FOR TODAY: We decree that we will have many afflictions in this life but God WILL deliver us out of them all! He said so! Walk like you are delivered!

Father, in Jesus' Name, it is a new day in the earth. Thank you for lifting our eyelids to behold your glory! You are gracious, Lord! Your compassions fail not. Great is thy faithfulness towards your people. Thank you bringing down every stronghold. Thank you for setting the captives free. Thank you for opening the heavens and pouring out your Spirit. Hallelujah! We praise you for your goodness towards mankind. Thank you for not cutting us off during the night. We could have gone into eternity, but you spared us another day. We give you glory, Lord. Bless those that are feeling weary. Give them strength. Lift their heavy burdens. Thank you for the garment of praise you have given to us for the spirit of heaviness. Let your anointing fall among us. In Jesus' Name, we thank you!

JUNE 28

Psalms 89:1

I will sing of the mercies of the LORD for ever: with my mouth will I make known thy faithfulness to all generations.

DECREE FOR TODAY: We decree that the God inside of us is not moved by the happenings of this world! We won't be moved, but we will STAND in spite of, and look through the eyes of God and think through the mind of God! Tell the devil so!

Father, in Jesus' Name, it is a day of thanksgiving and honoring you for being our High Priest, our Savior, Our deliverer, our strong tower, our defense, our battle axe, and our Mighty God! Nothing is too hard for you. Thank you for bringing down the high places in our lives. We are still here. Glory to God! Without your protection, we could have slipped into the world again! But your grace and divine favor has kept us afloat. You have provided a way of escape from every temptation. Though trials come and go, through storms try to uproot us, we thank you for keeping us grounded, settled and established on a firm foundation in a world full of confusion. But, you are greater than any force we may encounter! Your love heals our wounded spirits, broken hearts and restores us to a place of peace. Glory to God! We bless you, Lord God, in the Name of Jesus.

JUNE 29

Romans 8:18

For I reckon that the sufferings of this present time are not worthy to be compared with the glory which shall be revealed in us.

DECREE FOR TODAY: We decree that the Favor of God is upon us. Nothing can harm us! No weapon shall prosper!

Father, in Jesus' Name, thank you for your rich mercy and your great love wherewith you have loved us! Lord, while we were dead in our sins, you quickened us together in Christ! Thank you! You have raised us up together to sit in heavenly places in Christ and no weapon formed against us shall prosper! Thank you for the Blood of Jesus. You are our peace, our joy, our deliverer, our strong tower and everything that we need! Hallelujah! We will be strong in the Lord and in the power of his might, pulling down every stronghold that exalteth itself against the knowledge of God! We will use this great power you have put within to renew our minds daily so that we are not overwhelmed with the cares of this world! In Jesus' Name, we thank you Lord!

JUNE 30

1 Corinthians 15:57-58

But thanks be to God! He gives us the victory through our Lord Jesus Christ. Therefore, my dear brothers and sisters, stand firm. Let nothing move you. Always give yourselves fully to the work of the Lord, because you know that your labor in the Lord is not in vain.

DECREE FOR TODAY: We decree that we won't quit! We won't allow our minds to entertain defeat! Our God will fight for us! We will go forward!

Father, in Jesus' Name, we stand in the gap for those that seem to be losing hope and having a difficult time holding on. Strengthen them, Lord, with the power that you have put inside of us. For those that don't have the power, fill them as they repent, Lord. We speak to the minds and hearts of your people. Your record speaks for itself. Not one faileth! You have never lost a battle. Help us to understand that the battle is not ours, but it belongs to you. We lift up our hands now with a praise to you for those that have a spirit of heaviness. We speak joy, we speak peace and faith into their lives. Help all of us to trust you to the bitter end. For those that trust in the Lord shall be as Mt. Zion; they shall not be removed! Having done all, we can STAND! Thank you Lord, in Jesus' Name!

JULY 1

<u>Romans 8:38 – 39</u>

And I am convinced that nothing can ever separate us from God's love. Neither death nor life, neither angels nor demons, neither our fears for today nor our worries about tomorrow – not even the powers of hell can separate us from God's love.

DECREE FOR TODAY: We decree that we will not try to fight our battles. We will be still! The battles belong to the Lord! In quietness and confidence shall be our strength this day!

Father, in Jesus' Name, thank you for favor. Thank you for allowing us to dwell in the secret place of the Most High! You are the light of our salvation and the strength of our life! You are our Rock! You make us stand in the midst of situations that look devastating. You uphold us on the job, in the home, on the street, wherever we are! Your anointing stands tall! It is unbeatable! Thank you for our minds today, Lord, and assuring us that if we keep our minds on you, you will keep us in perfect peace. We rebuke the spirits of confusion and aggravation that follow us trying to pull us away from your hope. Satan desires to sift your people as wheat, but as you prayed for Peter when Satan desired to sift him, you have prayed for your people! Glory to God! We will walk in victory for the blood of Jesus has delivered us from the powers of the devil. Thank you Lord, in Jesus' Name!

JULY 2

<u>Galatians 2:20</u>

I am crucified with Christ: nevertheless I live; yet not I, but Christ liveth in me: and the life which I now live in the flesh I live by the faith of the Son of God, who loved me, and gave himself for me.

DECREE FOR TODAY: We decree that Jesus is the King of glory! The Lord Strong and Mighty! And if God be for us, who shall be able stand against us successfully! Nobody!

Father, in Jesus' Name, thank you for grace, mercy and strength. We bless you for the promise that you will be with us when we pass through the waters and rivers, and you won't let them overflow us; when we walk through the fire, and Lord some of us have fiery situations, you won't let us be burned. You are our Lord and there is none other. Thank you that you have never forsaken your people. Thank you for the anointing that breaks every yoke. We won't carry our burdens but we will cast them upon you. In you, Lord, is our hope, our deliverance, power to know that we can do all things through Christ that strengthens us. We won't allow the demons of heal to weary us. We won't allow the cares of this world to weigh us down. There is freedom in you. This is not our home, we are just passing through. Thank you for this great opportunity, Lord. We are looking unto the hills from whence cometh our help. Thank you Lord, in Jesus' Name!

JULY 3

Psalm 23:4

Yea, though I walk through the valley of the shadow of death, I will fear no evil: for thou art with me; thy rod and thy staff they comfort me.

DECREE FOR TODAY: I will rejoice in the Lord! No weapon formed against us shall prosper! Tell the devil God said so!

Father, in Jesus' Name, thank you for being the God of our strength and exceeding joy! You are our refuge and a very present help in the time of trouble. Hallelujah! You promised never to leave nor forsake us. All of your promises are yea and amen! We will trust you in spite of what we see, feel, think, or hear. We will clap our hands and shout with the voice of triumph for we know that the battle is not ours; it belongs to the Lord! We will be still and know that you are God! In the midst of our situations you will be exalted. You will bring down our high places and make our crooked places straight! That's your word, Lord. We receive it, we believe it and we thank you for it, in Jesus' Name!

JULY 4

Isaiah 40:31

But they that wait upon the LORD shall renew their strength; they shall mount up with wings as eagles; they shall run, and not be weary; and they shall walk, and not faint.

DECREE FOR TODAY: We decree that we will not allow ourselves to become angry at anything that the enemy has planned for us to day. We will shake it off! In Jesus' Name! Let the devil be mad alone!

Father, in Jesus' Name, thank you making us new creatures, allowing us to walk in the newness of life. Many of your people are going through some difficult moments, but none too difficult for you to handle. We are going to weather our storms. We won't try to outrun our storms, but we will allow you to deliver us – for you see dangers that are unseen to us. So we wait for you, Lord! We won't be bitter, we won't be angry, we won't allow malice and hatred to become a part of us because of our situations. Your word is our lifeboat! We will stay in the word, we will walk in the work, read it, and quote it until it becomes our daily way of life! You are our hiding place. You will preserve us from trouble. You will compass us about with songs of deliverance and we thank you, in Jesus' Name!

JULY 5

Psalm 119:9-11

How can a young man keep his way pure? By living according to your word. I seek you with all my heart; do not let me stray from your commands. I have hidden your word in my heart that I might not sin against you.

DECREE FOR TODAY: We decree that we will not allow our past to torment us. Forgetting those things that are behind, we will press toward the mark of the high calling of God which is in Christ Jesus! Tell the devil it is so!

Father, in Jesus' Name, we take time this day to give you thanks for who you are in our lives. We bless you for saving us – delivering us from the powers of darkness. Some of us you snatched from a dying situation, a destructive atmosphere, and drew us by your spirit into your marvelous kingdom. Glory to God, we thank you. Praise you for not allowing the enemy to destroy us. Thank you for opening our eyes. Hallelujah! We glorify you for this Joy that you have made available to give us strength. Praise you for the peace of God that surpasses all understanding. You are Lord and you reign above everything, making us royal, special people on our jobs, in our homes, on the street, wherever! You are in control and we walk humbly, but victoriously in this corrupt world. Thank you, Lord, in Jesus' Name!

JULY 6

<u>Habakkuk 3:19</u>

Yet I will rejoice in the LORD, I will joy in the God of my salvation. The LORD God is my strength, and he will make my feet like hinds' feet, and he will make me to walk upon mine high places.

DECREE FOR TODAY: We decree that we won't do anything to hinder the shift taking place in our lives! It's working for our good!

Father, in Jesus' Name, thank you for mercy! You could have cut us off, but you allowed us another day in the land of the living. We don't take it lightly, Lord. We are going to make good use of the time. We will walk worthy of you and pleasing. We'll be fruitful in every good work. We'll make an effort to increase in the knowledge of you. We will continue in the faith, grounded and settled. We won't be moved away from the hope of this great gospel! We won't be beguiled with enticing words. We will stand on your word, Lord! We will walk in you, rooted and building ourselves up and establishing ourselves in the faith. We are complete in you! Help us to realize that you have equipped us for this journey! Nothing, no weapon formed against us shall prosper! In Jesus' Name, we thank you!

JULY 7

<u>Matthew 25:40</u>

The King will reply, 'I tell you the truth, whatever you did for one of the least of these brothers of mine, you did for me.

DECREE FOR TODAY: We decree that God sees our lives as finished products! We need only let God take us through the earthly process! Nothing can stop Him!

Father, in Jesus' Name, thank you for this journey of life and giving us an opportunity to see and experience your glory, your miraculous works in the earth, your creation that man could never match! Hallelujah! Grateful that you took the time to mold man out of the dust of the earth and gave the dust the ability to know you in a way that no other creature could ever know you. Thank you for your presence that comforts our souls in the midst of the unknown and the known. To know you is to rest in peace, forgetting those things that are behind us and pressing forward. To know you is declared victory in every test and trial for you declared that many are the afflictions of the righteous but the Lord delivers them out of them ALL. Thank you Lord, in Jesus' Name,

JULY 8

Joshua 1:9

Have I not commanded you? Be strong and courageous. Do not be terrified; do not be discouraged, for the LORD your God will be with you wherever you go.

DECREE FOR TODAY: Having done ALL, we will be still and wait on the Lord!

Father, in the Name of Jesus thank you! Thank you, God, for all that you have done for us. No words could ever be formed to express our heartfelt gratefulness for your love that looks beyond our faults and sees our needs. Thank you for forgiveness today. We repent of all of our sins – our ways that are not like you, Lord, our thoughts that are not like you. Help us to forgive others as well as ourselves! We've not always come up to your standards, but we thank you for grace and mercy. Thank you for peace in knowing that you will never leave nor forsake your people. We pray for those that feel like giving up, throwing in the towel. You will give strength to the powerless and might to the faint! Thank you that there will be glory after this. In Jesus' Name, we thank you Lord!

JULY 9

Proverbs 1:7

The fear of the LORD is the beginning of knowledge: but fools despise wisdom and instruction.

DECREE FOR TODAY: We decree that we are FREE in Jesus. We will not be bound by no demon, no person, no religion, no,

NOTHING! We accept our freedom in Jesus' Name! Tell the devil it is so!

Father, in Jesus' Name, thank you for the opportunity to delight ourselves in you. If we do that, you have promised to give us the desires of our hearts, according to your divine will. We commit ourselves to you. We trust you. We will be still and know that you are God! Thank you for the power of the Holy Ghost that enables us to abound in hope. Thank you for helping your people to be righteous; for you promised that the righteous shall never be moved. The righteous is not afraid of bad news because he is trusting in God. We will not be afraid of sudden fear. We will rest in you for you promised your people sweet sleep. We will walk in our victory every day, knowing that you said we are more than conquerors through Christ. Thank you Lord, in Jesus' Name!

JULY 10

John 8:32
And ye shall know the truth, and the truth shall make you free.

DECREE FOR TODAY: We decree that our God is mighty! The devil has no power over us in the mind, the home, on the job, wherever! Tell him God said so!

Father, in the Name of Jesus thank you for a new day. Glory to God! Thank you for your faithfulness. You continue to make the sun rise daily. Oh how you have blessed us! Grateful that you have given us an opportunity to spend eternity with you. Regardless of our challenges, we will press on, Lord. Thank you, Jesus, for access to grace by faith which helps us to stand, in spite of! For in your presence is the fullness of joy! Victory is ours, in the home, on the job, or wherever we are! We are grateful for spiritual energy that overpowers whatever attacks our bodies, our minds, and our daily lives! And, Lord, we don't always see you at work, but our faith lets us know you are delivering, you are healing, and you are bringing about changes! No good thing will you withhold from them that walk upright! God, we thank you for peace of mind today in a world where there is no peace and we speak it into the lives of your people that don't have it. In Jesus' Name, we give you all the glory!

JULY 11

Psalm 19:14

Let the words of my mouth, and the meditation of my heart, be acceptable in thy sight, O LORD, my strength, and my redeemer.

DECREE FOR TODAY: We decree that we will be at peace with all men! If we are not at peace, we will make peace with all men for without it no man shall see the Lord!

Father, in Jesus' Name, thank you for being the Almighty God, the Great I Am in our lives. Nothing can compare to you, Lord. We honor the great power of the Holy Ghost that you have so freely given to your people to be saved, to face every challenge, to be victorious over every situation and most of all to be able to connect with you instantly because you dwell on the inside. Glory to God! We are encouraged to go forth, trusting you in spite of what we see or feel. Lord, you said we would go from strength to strength. We have the power to speak to the mountains in our lives and they have to move in due time! Thank you for keeping our minds in this disturbed world. We speak healing in sick bodies, renewed relationships, Lord. Mend broken marriages back together. Bless the children! Keep their hearts. Let the boldness of God be taught to them so they can survive the bullying going on. We thank you for it, in Jesus' Name!

JULY 12

1 Peter 5:6

Humble yourselves therefore under the mighty hand of God, that he may exalt you in due time.

DECREE FOR TODAY: We decree that we will plead the blood of Jesus against every aggravating spirit that crosses our paths today! God is bigger than aggravation! Yes He is!

Father, in Jesus' Name, thank you for being our Comforter the delight of our souls! We bless you for taking us through our trials. We are still here! Glory to God! We pray for the military. Lord, the soldiers that have sacrificed for us. We pray that you will strengthen those that are away from home. Keep their hearts from fear, God. On the battlefield, we pray they will call out to you for you are our protection. We pray for those that are wounded, in hospitals or wherever they may be, that you will show yourself strong and work a miracle for them, Lord. We pray for those bound by drugs and alcohol that we will remember they are some mother's and father's children. We command the devil to loose them, loose their minds. We pray for those that are in nursing homes doing well and those forgotten that children have abandoned. Comfort them Lord. We pray for the children and teachers in the classrooms. Keep them safe, Lord. Do it for your glory's sake. We thank you for it, in Jesus' Name!

JULY 13

Isaiah 12:2

Behold, God is my salvation; I will trust, and not be afraid: for the LORD JEHOVAH is my strength and my song; he also is become my salvation.

DECREEE FOR TODAY: We decree that we that we will not let the beating Jesus took for us be in vain! Oh no! We will STAND in spite of!

Father, in Jesus' Name, thank you for loving us, dying for us, shedding your precious blood for us! Grateful for this unexplainable love you have shown us! It is a day of thanksgiving Lord – giving you praise for all things. Lord, we bless you for giving your people a means to communicate around the world. Lord, many of us have been encouraged, renewed, enlightened, saved, and exposed to the many gifts that you have given your people around the world! The power of your word lifts us! Thank you that demons can't stop the technical means of spreading the gospel! You are the great technician! Thank you for the knowledge you have put inside of believers and unbelievers to accomplish your purpose. Thank you for the ability for your anointing to be felt through technical and written means. Hallelujah! Oh how powerful you are, Lord! You can do the impossible. We give you all the glory in Jesus' Name!

JULY 14

1 Thessalonians 5:18

In everything give thanks: for this is the will of God in Christ Jesus concerning you.

DECREE FOR TODAY: We decree that we are covered by the blood of Jesus and no weapon formed against us shall prosper! Tell the devil God said so!

Father, in Jesus' Name, we give you glory for this moment, whatever it beholds, it is working for our good according to your word! Thank you for preserving our souls. Thank you for mercy and grace following us all the days of our lives. Thank you for favor and forgiving us of our sins. You are our refuge and fortress. We trust in you Lord. No weapon formed against us shall prosper! Hallelujah! Help us to yield our thoughts to you for your thoughts are not like ours and your ways are not like our ways! Thank you for the Holy Ghost that steers us from our old ways, our old habits, and our evil thoughts! Glory! We will not walk to the devil's drum beat but we will stand, having done all stand on your word for it is sure. Help us to meditate on your word and to do it, then we shall prosper and have good success as Joshua did. Thank you Lord, in Jesus' Name!

JULY 15

Romans 8:1

There is therefore now no condemnation to them which are in Christ Jesus, who walk not after the flesh, but after the Spirit.

DECREE FOR TODAY: We decree that trouble doesn't last always. This too shall pass!

Father, in Jesus' Name, thank you for your protection day after day – keeping us, keeping our minds, and keeping our hearts from being overtaken by the evil of this life. Glory to God! Praise you for shielding us from the negative atmosphere and allowing our spirits to be able to rest in a positive atmosphere! Only you could do that, Lord. And when the enemy comes in like a flood, the Spirit of the Lord lifts up a standard against him! Thank you for continuing to purify the air that we breathe freely. Oh how we thank you that man has no opportunity to charge a fee for this oxygen that you supply us daily! You are in control, oh yes you are God! You still control who wakes up! Hallelujah! All power is in your hand! We believe you will answer our requests according to your divine will. We wait patiently for you knowing that your eyes run to and fro in the earth beholding the good and the evil. Thank you Lord, in Jesus' Name!

JULY 16

Romans 10:9

That if thou shalt confess with thy mouth the Lord Jesus, and shalt believe in thine heart that God hath raised him from the dead, thou shalt be saved.

DECREE: We decree that today we will use our minds as a sifter and sift everything that tries to disturb us! God is bigger than that!

Father, in Jesus' Name, thank you for the gospel that you have given us to comfort and establish us concerning our faith so that we are not moved by afflictions! Glory to God! Help us to walk in obedience to your word, Lord. For if we obey you, your word says your blessings will overtake us! Help us to wait patiently for you. Help us not to be distracted by the things of this world. Help us to use our minds as sifters to sift out negativity. Thank you for loving us and giving us hope in hopeless situations. Thank you covering us from harm and danger as we sleep through the night. We praise you for the angels that you have given us to take charge over us. Help us to hide your word in our hearts so that we won't sin against you, Lord. We shall live and not die! We thank you for it, in Jesus' Name!

JULY 17

Micah 6:8

He hath shewed thee, O man, what is good; and what doth the LORD require of thee, but to do justly, and to love mercy, and to walk humbly with thy God?

DECREE FOR TODAY: We decree that we will do everything in our power not to mention the devil's name today or what he is doing today! He doesn't deserve that much attention!

Father, in Jesus' Name, thank you that in your presence is the fullness of joy. And with joy shall we draw water out of the wells of salvation. We pray that those that don't have joy that they will obey your word that says leap for joy! You promised that those that sow in tears shall reap in joy! Their weeping may endure for a night, but Joy is coming in the morning! Glory to

God! Lord, we pray for the wounded in spirit. You heal the broken hearted and bind up their wounds! We pray for those crying out for whatever reason that they will grab hold of faith, for it will carry them through the worst of storms. You promised the disciples that if they asked anything in your Name, their joy would be full. Help us to remember the power that is in your Name, Jesus! Hallelujah! We thank you for the Name in Jesus' Name!

JULY 18

<u>Psalm 37:1</u>

Fret not thyself because of evildoers, neither be thou envious against the workers of iniquity.

DECREE FOR TODAY: We decree that greater is the God that is in us than the devil that is in the world – in our homes, on the job, on the street, wherever!

Father, in Jesus' Name, thank you for waking us up this morning. Many did not wake up but your grace, mercy, and compassions continue to be extended to us. Thank you for the things that you provide for us. Thank you, Lord, for water. If we didn't have it, we would thirst to death. You continue to fill the oceans and rivers so that they don't run dry. Glory to God. Help us not to be wasteful, Lord, for there are so many that don't have even clean water. We drink what want and we throw the rest out! Glory to God! Help us to be mindful and appreciate your provisions. Thank you for the heartbeat that you continue to monitor day after day, for millions around the world, that keeps us alive. Hallelujah! Oh how grateful we are, Lord. Thank you for the Blood of Jesus that has never lost its power and continues to cover us. We bless you today, and we thank you for all things, in Jesus' Name!

JULY 19

<u>Psalm 51:10</u>

Create in me a clean heart, O God; and renew a right spirit within me.

DECREEE FOR TODAY: We decree that we CAN do all things through Christ that strengthens us! We will!

Father, in Jesus' Name, oh how we love you, Lord! Hallelujah! We give you the highest praise Lord! You are worthy! Thank you for the opportunity to talk to you through this miraculous means of prayer. We don't always have to feel you nor see your actions but by faith we know that you hear us. And, God, you promised that if we know that you hear us, we can ask you anything in your Name and you will do it according to your divine will! Glory to God! Today, we know you are answering; some are going to receive miracles, healings, deliverances, and provisions. It is due time today for some. And for those that are still waiting, we have your promise that we will reap if we don't faint! You are awesome, Lord! Thank you for the joy that you have put inside of us – joy that overrides pain, overrides doubt, and overrides circumstances! Thank you, Lord, in Jesus' Name!

JULY 20

John 14:19

Yet a little while and the world will see me no more, but you will see me. Because I live, you also will live.

DECREE FOR TODAY: We decree that the only thing that really matters in this life is that we please God! All else is worthless - energy wasted!

-

Father, in Jesus' Name, we give you glory, we give you honor, we praise you for being the Mighty God, the God that sits high and looks low. Thank you that your eyes run to and fro beholding the good and the evil in the earth. Your compassions fail not! Hallelujah! Nothing in this earth can out-power you. Thank you for not allowing man to control the sun, Lord, for some of us would be in darkness, left without the ability to move. Thank you for the freedom in the Spirit, for in the Spirit there are no big "I"s and little "U"s. All of us have the right to get the same healing, the same deliverance, the same authority over demons, for you said John the Baptist was the greatest prophet born of a woman, but the least of us in your kingdom is greater than him. Thank you that no matter what our situation is, we can use our faith to conquer, wherever we are. Thank you Lord, in Jesus' Name!

JULY 21

Psalm 34:18

The LORD is nigh unto them that are of a broken heart; and saveth such as be of a contrite spirit.

DECREE FOR TODAY: We decree that we will allow ourselves to be armed with the strength of God – we will go forth this day conquering in the Spirit, not in the flesh! The Spirit is greater!

Father, in Jesus' Name, we thank you for your Word! It brings life into our spirits. It is like a hammer that breaketh the rock in pieces. It assures us that though we may go through many things in this life, we are more than conquerors. Sometimes persecuted, but not forsaken. Sometimes cast down, but not destroyed! Thank you for building our spirit man with the power that is above all powers! Glory to God! Nothing shall separate us from your love Lord! No persecution, no famine, no hardship! Oh, Lord God! Thank you for putting within us the determination to endure, in spite of what comes our way. Lord, we are grateful for this joy, this unspeakable joy. And though weeping may endure for a night, joy comes in the morning! Our soul rejoices in the God of our salvation! Oh, Jesus, how we appreciate your faithfulness to us in the midst of a crooked world! Thank you Lord, in Jesus' Name!

JULY 22

John 16:33

I have told you these things, so that in me you may have peace. In this world you will have trouble. But take heart! I have overcome the world.

DECREE FOR TODAY: We decree that we will not allow demons to wound our spirits! God has already defeated the devil! It's written! Our spirits will strut like the King's kids today! For if the inward man is made glad, so will the outer be! Glory to God!

Father, in Jesus' Name, we bless you today, Lord. There is none in the earth greater than you. You have the power to do all things, including those things that are impossible to man. Glory! Bless your people today. Some have been waiting a long time for a change, for healing, for deliverance, but your time is the right time. You promised never to leave us nor forsake us. Your word is true. Increase the faith of your people, Lord. Increase strength. Increase boldness. Increase endurance in the minds; it all begins in our minds. Help us to yield them to you. For when we have the mind of Christ, we can face every obstacle and every demon with a winning attitude, because you never lose. Help us to delight ourselves in your statues and not forget your word, Lord; for all of your promises are yea and amen. In Jesus' Name, we thank you!

JULY 23

Isaiah 53:5

But he was wounded for our transgressions, he was bruised for our iniquities: the chastisement of our peace was upon him; and with his stripes we are healed.

DECREE FOR TODAY: We decree that we will not participate in any conversation that will destroy our FRIENDS or FAMILY in the home, on the job, on the street, wherever! The devil is a liar! God is bigger than that!

Father, in Jesus' Name, thank you for coming to earth in human form and dying for us at Calvary. The Blood is precious to us, Lord. It will never lose its power. It was shed for all mankind, though some have ignored your great sacrifice! Some refuse to worship you. But, we thank you for giving us the spirit to respond to your call. We won't let you down, Lord. We are going to wear this world like a loose garment. We will not be deceived by the devil, for we are not ignorant concerning his devices. We won't let people control us and take away this liberty that you have given us. We will walk in victory. Every trial is our stepping stone to a closer walk and a deeper knowledge of you. By faith we see our prayers answered. Thank you Lord, in Jesus' Name!

JULY 24

Matthew 6:9-13

Our Father which art in heaven, Hallowed be thy name. Thy kingdom come. Thy will be done in earth, as it is in heaven. Give us

this day our daily bread. And forgive us our debts, as we forgive our debtors. And lead us not into temptation, but deliver us from evil: For thine is the kingdom, and the power, and the glory, for ever. Amen.

DECREE FOR TODAY: We decree that we will not listen to the whispers of demons nor allow them to influence us! God is bigger than that!

Father, in Jesus' Name, we give you glory for who you are. If you never do another thing for us in the earth, you've done enough at Calvary to take care of it all! Hallelujah! Because of Calvary, we are healed, we are delivered from the powers of darkness, we can sit together with you in high places, we can call those things that are not as though they were, and we can speak to the situations that sound like roaring waves and command peace! Glory to God! Hallelujah for the power of the Holy Ghost. Thank you for this treasure in earthen vessels that the excellency of the power may be of God and not us! We are just the dust of the earth, clay molded and shaped by you for your glory! Thank you for the opportunity to come from dirt and become children of God. In Jesus' Name, we thank you Lord!

JULY 25

Isaiah 43:1-3

Fear not: for I have redeemed thee, I have called thee by thy name; thou art mine. When thou passest through the waters, I will be with thee; and through the rivers, they shall not overflow thee: when thou walkest through the fire, thou shalt not be burned.

DECREE FOR TODAY: We decree that we will not allow our today to be miserable because of something Satan said to us yesterday. God is bigger than that!

Father, in Jesus' Name, thank you for keeping us during the night. We are so grateful that your mercy and grace stays with us day after day. Thank you Lord for protecting your people from harm and danger. We are resting under the shadow of your wings. We pray for those cities experiencing violence, killings and all kinds of demonic activity Lord. Cover your people. Keep our children safe in this wicked world. We pray for those at war, fighting to protect us. Keep them strong, Lord. We pray for their encouragement. Bless their families that are left behind. Thank you for the power of endurance in whatever our situations may be, for no trial or test has lasted forever. Many are the afflictions of the righteous you promised to deliver them out of ALL! We will recover ALL. Thank you Lord, in Jesus' Name.

JULY 26

Isaiah 30:21

And thine ears shall hear a word behind thee, saying, This is the way, walk ye in it, when ye turn to the right hand, and when ye turn to the left.

DECREE FOR TODAY: We decree that we will make every attempt to sift thoughts that come to our mind so that evil thoughts will not enter our hearts! God is bigger than that!

Father, in Jesus' Name, thank you for strengthening our inner man with your might by your Spirit Lord! Glory to God! We appreciate you dwelling within our hearts by faith, giving us the ability to be rooted and grounded in love. Thank you for helping us to know your love that passeth knowledge so that we can be filled with all the fullness of God. We know, Lord, that you are able to do exceeding abundantly above all that we ask or think according to this great power that worketh in us. Thank you for the power, Lord! We won't grieve you. We will put away bitterness, wrath, anger, evil speaking and malice. We will rejoice in you, knowing that better is coming. We thank you for it in Jesus' Name!

JULY 27

Romans 5:3 – 5

And not only so, but we glory in tribulations also: knowing that tribulation worketh patience; And patience, experience; and experience, hope!

DECREE FOR TODAY: We decree that we will not allow the enemy to occupy any space in our atmosphere today! When we see him coming, in our spirit we will plead the blood of Jesus against him! It's our space in God! He has no right to enter!

Father, in Jesus' Name, thank you for your rich mercy and your great love towards us. You have raised us up from our sins, our own ways, our own thoughts, and made us to sit together in heavenly places in Christ Jesus.

Gory to God! We are your workmanship. At one time we were aliens, and while we were yet sinners, you died for us. The cross has made the difference. We won't forget the Blood, Lord, that you shed at Calvary. The Blood still works! We will plead your Blood today over everything that is not like you. There is power in your Blood. It was not in vain. We appreciate your sacrifice, and we will use this great power that you have given us to overcome every obstacle no matter how tall or strong it may be. For in you, all power is available to us. Thank you, Lord, in Jesus' Name!

JULY 28

Philippians 4:13
I can do all things through Christ who strengthens me.

DECREE FOR TODAY: We decree that we will not allow our minds to be cluttered with things that don't really matter! God is bigger than that! Rest in the Lord!

Father, in Jesus' Name, we speak peace on the jobs, in the home, and wherever your people are right now! You have given us authority over every demon! None is too strong for us to handle because of the Holy Ghost within! Glory to God! We plead the blood of Jesus over the minds of your people! Help them not to fear man on the job, in the home, wherever! We have the power over the devil! Glory to God! We will walk in victory. We will lift our spirits above those that are attacking us mentally! You are all power God! We thank you Lord, in Jesus' Name!

JULY 29

Philippians 4:6 -7
Be careful for nothing; but in every thing by prayer and supplication with thanksgiving let your requests be made known unto God. And the peace of God, which passeth all understanding, shall keep your hearts and minds through Christ Jesus.

DECREE FOR TODAY: We decree that we will not fear nor worry about the unknown. We serve a God that knows all! He is bigger than the unknown!

Father, in Jesus' Name, that you for making us to lie down in green pastures. Thank you for rest, Lord. Thank you for guiding us with your counsel. In the midst of uncertainties, you will lead us in paths that we have not known. You will make darkness light before us, and crooked places straight! Glory to God! You give light to them that sit in darkness, and you guide our feet into the way of peace. Thank you! You promised and you have guided us into truth. Thank you for the Comforter, the Holy Ghost! Continue to lead us in righteousness. Teach us to do your will, for you are our God! You are our divine leader in difficult places. Remember us, Lord. We thank you, in Jesus' Name!

JULY 30

2 Timothy 2:7

Consider what I say; and the Lord give thee understanding in all things.

DECREE FOR TODAY: We decree that he that hath begun a good work in us will complete it! No demon traveling the earth, wherever, can stop it!

Father, in Jesus' Name, thank you for faith! Glory to God! It's something we don't see, we can't touch it, but you through your power have put it, a belief, inside of us. We can use it to speak to mountains, even if it is only the size of a mustard seed. We know we can't please you without faith, Lord. You saved us by grace through faith and have justified us! Help us to realize the value of faith. By faith kingdoms were subdued, by faith Israel crossed the Red Sea on DRY land, by faith the Jericho wall fell. So, Lord, by faith we are speaking to every situation in our lives. By faith, we claim healing, deliverance, and salvation for our loved ones and prosperity. Whatever we need, by faith we receive it, Lord, and we thank you for it, in Jesus' Name!

JULY 31

Matthew 11:28 – 30

Come unto me, all ye that labour and are heavy laden, and I will give you rest. Take my yoke upon you, and learn of me; for I am meek and lowly in heart: and ye shall find rest unto your souls. For my yoke is easy, and my burden is light.

DECREE FOR TODAY: We decree that we will not walk around with the spirits of discouragement, confusion, uncertainty, fear,

doubt, whatever! Not today! Jesus came that we might have life and more abundantly! We will walk in victory!

Father, in Jesus' Name, we come boldly to your throne today. Some of us are joyous, some of us have bowed down heads, some of us are sick in the body, some of us are discouraged and stressed, but whatever state we are in, help us to be content. You give us laughter; you are the lifter of the bowed down heads. You are our Jehovah Rophe, our healer, and you are our hope and our deliverer from ALL of our afflictions! Hallelujah! We have come to you, the right one! Thank you for being the Mighty God, the Prince of Peace! Everything is under your authority. Demons tremble at your Name! Hallelujah! We love the Name of Jesus, for it is our strong tower, and we can run into your Name and find safety. Bless us today, Lord, spiritually so that we can learn how to soar in you, above every storm. Thank you Lord, in Jesus' Name!

AUGUST 1

Psalm 127:1

Except the LORD build the house, they labour in vain that build it: except the LORD keep the city, the watchman waketh but in vain.

DECREE FOR TODAY: We decree that our situations are not hopeless! We know that whatever is wrong, God can fix it and He will!

Father, in Jesus' Name, we appreciate the things you have done for us. Thank you for grace. Your favor covers us in an unjust world. Your Spirit within gives us authority over the powers of darkness. Glory to God! Your gift of discernment allows us to see behind faces. You prepare us spiritually to deal with the everyday happenings and to still have the peace of God no matter what it brings. Help us to remain steadfast, unmovable, always abounding in you, Lord! Help us to renew our minds, realizing that All Power is in you, and you in us makes us unstoppable. Our delight is in you. You declared the righteous shall live by faith! We shall live and not die, in Jesus' Name!

AUGUST 2

James 1:12

Blessed is the man that endureth temptation: for when he is tried, he shall receive the crown of life, which the Lord hath promised to them that love him.

DECREE FOR TODAY: We decree that we will create an atmosphere of peace and not allow the devil to invade our space on the job, in the home, wherever! Not today! The blood of Jesus is against the demons! Yes Lord!

Father, in Jesus' Name, oh how grateful we are for one more day in the land of the living. We don't take it lightly, Lord. We thank you for your promise to give power to the faint and for those that have no might you will increase their strength. Thank you for healing the broken in heart and binding up their wounds. The world is in trouble but you are still the same. Those that put their trust in you shall not be afraid. In quietness and confidence shall be our strength! You are our God that giveth beauty for ashes, the oil of joy for mourning and the garment of praise for the spirit of heaviness. Glory! Thank you for the assurance that better is the ending of a thing than the beginning. We give you glory in Jesus' Name!

AUGUST 3

Romans 12:14

Bless them which persecute you: bless, and curse not.

DECREE FOR TODAY: We decree that Today we will take our faith and stretch it tightly, strongly over every problem we have so that doubt can't creep in! For without faith, we cannot please God!

Father, in Jesus' Name, thank you for another chance to give you some glory for who you are. Oh how we love you, Jesus. Thank you for protecting us through the night, covering us while we slept from all harm and danger. We pray for those that are facing trying times, which includes all of us in some way. You have not given us the spirit of fear, but one of power, love and a sound mind. And Lord the enemy is running to and fro trying to put the demonic spirit of fear in your people's minds, but we rebuke that demon and command it to get out of the atmosphere. You promised us peace that surpasses all understanding. Help us to remember that you are not a man that you should lie, but if you said it, it shall come to pass. By faith we will pull down every stronghold. We will live in the power of your word for everything is going down but your Word! Thank you for the ability to speak to our mountains; they must come down in Jesus' Name, we give you glory!

AUGUST 4

<u>Ecclesiastes 3:14</u>

I know that, whatsoever God doeth, it shall be forever: nothing can be put to it, nor any thing taken from it.

DECREE FOR TODAY: We decree that every word of God is true!

Father, in Jesus' Name, we are so grateful to you for allowing yourself to be beaten, mistreated, and nailed to a cross for a dying world of souls that you love. We have all come short of your glory, Lord. Forgive us! Oh how grateful we are, Lord, for your grace and mercy. Thank you for life and thank you for keeping the earth intact. Thank you for making the seas and oceans obey your voice and remain beyond the sand so that we are not drowned. Oh, Lord, thank you for your power that you so graciously have given to us to stand against every obstacle. Help us to realize that we are walking around with the greatest power in the world on the inside of us that can handle everything on the job, in the home, and wherever! Hallelujah! The God that spoke the world into being, the God that created everything and owns the world and everything in it is alive within us! Oh Glory to God for your power, Lord. Help us to realize who we are in you. Thank you Lord, in Jesus' Name!

AUGUST 5

<u>Hebrews 11:1</u>

Now faith is the substance of things hoped for, the evidence of things not seen.

DECREE FOR TODAY: We decree that the spirits of unforgiveness and bitterness that may try to attack us are bound in the Name of Jesus! God is bigger than that!

Father, in the Name of Jesus, we call your Name today. Jesus, your Name is a strong tower and the righteous runneth into it and is safe. Lord, we lift up those today that are heavy laden. Thank you for the garment of praise for the spirit of heaviness. We take authority over the demons assigned over our cities. We plead the blood of Jesus against them and their planned activities. Every attack is rebuked. We rebuke fear today. We rebuke anxiety, doubt, discouragement and depression. We speak peace into the atmosphere! Every high place must come down. Every crooked place will be made straight. Let your anointing flow, Lord. Dispatch the warring angels into the homes where the demons of confusion are raging. Let the peace of God that surpasses all understanding prevail in the lives of your people. Thank you Lord, in Jesus' Name!

AUGUST 6

John 10:10

The thief cometh not, but for to steal, and to kill, and to destroy: I am come that they might have life, and that they might have it more abundantly.

DECREE FOR TODAY: We decree that we will mentally bind every demonic attack against our minds today. The discouraging, negative, depressing, offensive demons are bound in Jesus' Name! God is bigger than that!

Father, in Jesus' Name, we bless you Lord. You are worthy of all the praises. Thank you for giving us faith, for it is the victory that overcometh the world. We will be content with the things that you have given us. We won't complain. We will not be anxious, but in everything by prayer and supplication with thanksgiving we will make our requests known to you, Lord. Thank you that all that labor and are heavy laden and come to you, you will give rest. We won't fear, for you are with us. We won't be dismayed for you are our God! You will strengthen us. You will help us! You have promised that those that cry unto you, Lord, in their trouble, you will hear and save them out of their distresses. We are confident that you began a good work in our lives and you will complete it until the day of Jesus Christ. We thank you for the hope that lies within us, Lord in Jesus' Name!

AUGUST 7

__Proverbs 3:24__

When you lie down, you will not be afraid; when you lie down, your sleep will be sweet.

DECREE FOR TODAY: We decree that we will not be distracted this day by the news, by co-workers, neighbors, friends, family, nor the devil! No one! We will keep our minds stayed on the Lord – then is perfect peace guaranteed!

Father, in Jesus' Name, thank you for sanctification. We sanctify you in our hearts. Help us to always be ready to give an answer to every man that asks us a reason of the hope that is in us. Thank you for hope, faith and love that abideth, knowing that the greatest of these is love. Thank you for the word of God that is a source for us. Those things that were written aforetime were written for our learning. Through our patience, Lord, and comfort of the scriptures, we would have hope. Glory to God! You are awesome! You are mighty! You are wonderful. Thank you for this written word. It is food for our souls. It lifts, it delivers, it heals, it encourages, and it has all of the answers that we need. Thank you, in Jesus' Name!

AUGUST 8

__Matthew 6:19-21__

Lay not up for yourselves treasures upon earth, where moth and rust doth corrupt, and where thieves break through and steal: But lay up for yourselves treasures in heaven!

DECREE FOR TODAY: God is unstoppable! So that makes us unstoppable in the home, on the job, wherever! Satan can't stop us! God in us is bigger than that! Say it today – I'm unstoppable!

Father, in Jesus' Name, thank you for this moment in time in this life and for granting us the privilege to spend eternity in a better life. Hallelujah! But while we are here Lord, our faith is in you, our hope is in you, and everything that we need is in you Lord! We will stand! Having done all, we will stand, Lord. You have built our minds to endure whatever comes against us. Every day, we will renew our minds. We will lean on you to let you think through us. For your thoughts are not like our thoughts nor are your ways like ours. We give over to you our selfish attitudes, our have it my way or no way attitudes, and our impatience to let you handle things. We surrender it all to you. We will not give place to the devil in our minds, our homes, on our jobs, wherever because we have your promise that the desire of the righteous shall be granted. Thank you, Lord, in Jesus' Name!

AUGUST 9

Mark 8:38

Whosoever therefore shall be ashamed of me and of my words in this adulterous and sinful generation; of him also shall the Son of man be ashamed, when he cometh in the glory of his Father with the holy angels.

DECREE FOR TODAY: We decree that we will walk in victory today! Looking unto Jesus in spite of what we see in the home, on the job, on the street, wherever! We will not fear! God is bigger than fear!

Father, in Jesus' Name, thank you for always being with us, even unto the end. We will not take thought for tomorrow for your word says tomorrow shall take thought for the things of itself. We will seek the kingdom of God and your righteousness, which guarantees that all these things shall be added unto us. We will not be anxious for anything, but in everything by prayer and supplication with thanksgiving, we will let our requests be made known unto you. We will abide in your peace that passeth all understanding which comes with a promise that our hearts and minds will be kept through Christ Jesus. Hallelujah! Heaviness in the heart of man maketh the heart to stoop, but a good word maketh it glad! Thank you for your word that says your plans towards us are good and not evil and to give us an expected end. Thank you Lord, in Jesus' Name!

AUGUST 10

Romans 12:1-2

I beseech you therefore, brethren, by the mercies of God, that ye present your bodies a living sacrifice, holy, acceptable unto God!

DECREE FOR TODAY: We decree that we will renew our minds to think positive like God thinks, in the home, on the job, on the street, wherever!

Father, in Jesus' Name, thank you for being our refuge and strength! We will be still and know that you are God! You are our confidence and will keep us in perfect peace as long as we keep our minds stayed on thee. You came that we might have life, and that we might have it more abundantly. You have not given us the spirit of fear in the home, on the job, wherever but of power, love and a sound mind! Thank you Lord. Order our steps in your word! We won't be dismayed. You will strengthen us, yea you will help us through this journey. Thank you for daily loading us with benefits; you are the God of our salvation. Thank you for forgiving us of all of our iniquities. You are our God that healeth all diseases, broken hearts and bind up wounds. Thank you for delivering us from people that want to control us. We have the power over the devil for greater is he that is in us than he that is in the world. Thank you Lord, in Jesus' Name!

AUGUST 11

Philippians 3:7-8

But what things were gain to me, those I counted loss for Christ.

DECREE FOR TODAY: We decree that this day negativity is defeated. NOT going to receive it. Oh No! Not today! God is bigger than that!

Father, in Jesus' Name, how great is your goodness that is laid up for those that fear you, that reverence you Lord! Thank you for the angels you have assigned to camp round about us. You are our refuge and strength. You are our present help in the time of trouble. You have given us your word to preserve our going out and our coming in. Thank you, Lord. We will not be afraid of sudden fear neither of the desolate of the wicked. You are our confidence. When the enemy comes in like a flood, the spirit of the Lord will lift up a standard against him! Glory to God! You are our Passover! We apply the blood to our lives, our homes, our jobs, our children, whatever and wherever! The Blood still works! Thank you for provision. You promised to supply every need according to your riches in glory by Christ Jesus. We believe it. We thank you for it, in Jesus' Name!

AUGUST 12

Revelation 19:9
And they overcame him by the blood of the Lamb, and by the word of their testimony; and they loved not their lives unto the death

DECREEE FOR TODAY: We decree that we will let go of our hurting past and unforgiveness! We will not take it mentally into our future! God in us is bigger than that!

Father, in Jesus' Name, we bless you. We will not forget all of your benefits. We enter the gates with thanksgiving and your courts with praise for who you are in our lives! We are grateful for being received into your kingdom that cannot be shaken! You have done great things for us whereof we are glad. You miraculously woke us up this morning and gave us a mind that can recall the things that we need to remember. Hallelujah! This great mystery of your power residing on the inside of us has equipped us for the storms and battles of this life. Thank you that we need only to stand still and see the salvation of the Lord. We need not fight for the battle belongs to you! Thank for this great power of the Holy Ghost that battles negativity and always produces positive results. Thank you for the promise that weeping may endure for a night but joy is coming in the morning. You are not slack concerning your promises. Help us to wait on you and be of a good courage and you will strengthen our hearts. Thank you Lord, in Jesus' Name!

AUGUST 13

Proverbs 31:28
Her children arise up, and call her blessed; her husband also, and he praiseth her.

DECREE FOR TODAY: We decree that nothing shall interfere with our peace! Keeping our minds stayed on the Lord will keep us in perfect peace!

Father, in Jesus' Name, we give you glory for a brand new day. Help us to cherish each moment for as every moment passes, it brings us closer to your coming back to get your people. Thank you for sending the Comforter, the Holy Ghost, to keep us while you have gone away to prepare a place for us Lord. Bless today. You are nigh unto those that are of a broken heart and save such as be of a contrite spirit. You are nigh unto all that call upon you in truth. Thank you that we can abide in you and ask you for anything according to your divine will and you will do it. That's your word Lord. We believe it. We stand on it. We won't lean to our own understanding. In all things that we encounter on this day, help us to remember to acknowledge you. Every Jericho wall in our lives must come down. We declare it to be so and we thank you, in Jesus' Name!

AUGUST 14

Psalms 88:2

Let my prayer come before thee: incline thine ear unto my cry

DECREE FOR TODAY: We decree that knowing who we are in Christ makes the difference in our lives! No demon can overpower the Christ in us! Know it! Put it in your mind! Put it in your spirit.

Father, in Jesus' Name, it is a day of thanksgiving for who you are. Thank you for being mighty in our lives. You are the strength of our joy, our peace, our provider. You are everything that we need! Thank you! We lift your Name on high Jesus! Thank you for the Word of God that gives us hope! Thank you for the blind man that you healed, which gives hope to those seeking your face for sight. Thank you for raising the dead. It gives hope for us in our dead situations. We can't thank you enough for shedding your blood. Because of it, we live, we move and have our being! Glory! In everything Lord, we are learning to say thank you! Whatever comes our way, thank you! All things are working together for our good! We will walk by faith, trusting in the God that created this world and lives inside of us. Thank you for taking up residence in us, delivering us from ourselves, our habits, and our old ways! In Jesus' Name, we thank you Lord!

AUGUST 15

Ephesians 2:8

For by grace are ye saved through faith; and that not of yourselves: it is the gift of God.

DECREE FOR TODAY: We decree that Nothing can stand against us successfully! Tell the devil God says No weapon! No weapon formed against us shall prosper!

Father, in Jesus' Name, oh what a privilege it is to be given an opportunity to come into your presence with our requests, though we have all come short of your glory. You remain the same. You look beyond our faults – our disobedience, our failure to acknowledge you in all of our ways. You remain faithful. Even in our battles, Lord sometimes we are looking at the circumstances instead of looking inward to the God that can do anything. Help us to stay dressed with the whole armour of God so that we can stand against the wiles of the devil. Help us to lay aside the sword of the tongue and pick up the Word of God, which is the sword of the Spirit. Live through us so that our lives and minds are renewed daily and our speech will be with grace and not anger. We are new creatures in you; behold old things are passed away. Thank you for the strength of endurance in a world of uncertainty and the assurance that though our afflictions may be many, you will deliver us out of them all. In Jesus' Name, we thank you, Lord!

AUGUST 16

Proverbs 3: 5-6

Trust in the Lord with all thine heart, and lean not unto thine own understanding. In all thy ways acknowledge Him, and He shall direct thy paths.

DECREE FOR TODAY: We decree that we will plead the Blood of Jesus for victory on the job, in the home, wherever we are! It still works!

Father, in Jesus' Name, thank you for making today a time that fulfilled tomorrow for some that have been waiting for a tomorrow! A new beginning. A time to leave the past in the past and focus on the now. Our light afflictions are but for a moment and are working for us an eternal weight of glory! Thank you, God, for our trials for they produce a steadfastness in us. We are not surprised when these fiery trials come to test us as though some strange thing has happened to us. Help us to remember that we are sharing in your sufferings. When they drove those nails in your hands and feet, you took the pain, for us! You didn't get up and say forget it. No! Lord, you went through; how much more about us! Continue to strengthen us for this journey so that with everything that comes against us, we can say, it won't prosper and believe it in our spirits. Thank you for the anointing that fights the demonic forces we encounter. In Jesus' Name, we thank you Lord!

AUGUST 17

Matthew 24:34-35

Verily I say unto you, This generation shall not pass, till all these things be fulfilled. Heaven and earth shall pass away, but my words shall not pass.

DECREE FOR TODAY: We decree that the struggle is over!

Father, in Jesus' Name, thank you for the victory over all things. We bless you Lord. Your grace and mercy has kept us, covered us, and protected us because they are following us every day. Thank you Lord! Some of us have been through rough places but you brought us out. Some of us are still in rough places but we have your promise that if we have the faith the size of a grain of a mustard seed, we can speak to the mountain and it will move. We speak to sickness in the body and command it to go NOW in the Name of Jesus. We speak to the low in spirit and encourage them to wait on the Lord! We trust you Lord. We cast all of our burdens upon you. Thank you for faith, thank you for strength, thank you for drying our tears, and lifting our bowed down heads. Glory to God! We go forward knowing that when you speak, demons tremble. We rest in you Lord and we know that whatever we are in, we're coming out, in Jesus' Name, we thank you!

AUGUST 18

Luke 10:19

I give unto you power to tread on serpents and scorpions, and over all the power of the enemy: and nothing shall by any means hurt you.

DECREE FOR TODAY: We decree that there will be glory after this!

Father, in Jesus' Name, thank you for another day of life which is a miracle that you have given to all of us. Thank you for lifting our eyelids again to behold the beauty of your creation. Thank you for keeping us in perfect peace in the midst of a world full of confusion. Because of you, we won't allow our hearts to be troubled though we may be troubled on every side. We won't be distressed! Your Spirit in us brings life, gives us joy, overcoming power, power to walk on demon's heads, power to speak to our mountains and watch them come down. Thank you for your strength that enables us to wait on you Lord! Bless the young people today Lord. Many are going through things created by demons. We rebuke the satanic influence trying to destroy them. We plead the blood over them. Let your anointing cover them Lord. Draw them to you and we pray they will respond. We thank you for all things in Jesus' Name!

AUGUST 19

Psalm 119:11
Thy word have I hid in mine heart, that I might not sin against thee.

DECREE FOR TODAY: We decree that God is in control. We will not fear!

Father, in Jesus' Name, it is a day of thanksgiving for who you are and what you are to us and in our daily lives! We give you glory for the wounds you suffered for our transgressions, the bruises you received for our iniquities. Thank you for peace! Thank you for enduring the beatings and taking the stripes for our healing! Hallelujah! Thank you that when we pass through the waters and rivers – the difficult and great trials of this life, you don't allow them to drown us. When our battles get heated, you don't allow us to get burned. You have taught us that the battle is not ours, it belongs to the Lord! Thank you for the strength to Stand against the wiles of the devil. Hallelujah! When things seem like thorns in our flesh, your grace is sufficient for us. We go forward, knowing that ALL things are working together for our good and we will recover all. Thank you Lord God, in Jesus' Name!

AUGUST 20

1 John 3:18
My little children, let us not love in word, neither in tongue; but in deed and in truth.

DECREE FOR TODAY: We decree that we live, we move and we have our being in Christ! Nothing else shall move us!

Father, in Jesus' Name, we are grateful for your love. There is no one like you. And Lord whatever we do, we will do it heartily unto you and not for man's glory. You are our Blessed Hope! You are able to do exceedingly abundantly above all that we ask or even think! Glory! We will trust you Lord. We have been crucified with you. This life that we now live is by faith in you Jesus! Thank you for loving us and giving yourself for us. Your Blood has redeemed us and delivered us from the powers of Satan. The Blood covers! For those that are discouraged, sad, losing hope, and at wits end, we plead the blood over their lives today. Satan, take your hands off God's people. We have power over the demonic forces because of the Blood. We rebuke depression! We rebuke discouragement! Get out of the lives of God's people! The Blood of Jesus is against you spirits of evil! We will get up from where we are today and walk in our victory and we thank you for it Lord, in Jesus' Name!

AUGUST 21

Proverbs 30:5

Every word of God is pure: he is a shield unto them that put their trust in him.

DECREE FOR TODAY: We decree that the just shall live by faith! We will live and not die!

Father, in Jesus' Name, thank you for the favor of God that is upon your people. We know that you work all things according to the counsel of your own will. You don't consult with man. Hallelujah! Your favor is for a lifetime. Weeping may endure for a night but joy is promised to come in the morning. Thank you that our light affliction is but for a moment. We pray for those that seem faint in the moment. Strengthen, Lord. Send help from your sanctuary. Help us to remember your word that the righteous shall never be moved. We are not afraid of bad news! That's your word! We will trust you Lord. We won't let our hearts be troubled! You will daily bear us up and when the enemy comes in like a flood, the Spirit of the Lord will lift up a standard against him! You will deliver us from the snare of the fowler and the pestilences on the job, in the home, on the street – wherever we encounter them, Lord! Thank you for the secret place in you. In Jesus' Name!

AUGUST 22

John 14:1

Let not your heart be troubled: ye believe in God, believe also in me.

DECREE FOR TODAY: We decree that we will hold our peace!

Father, in Jesus' Name, we come humbly and at the same time boldly before your throne because you have given us permission to do so. We know we can't do anything without you, but with you, we can do all things! Hallelujah! We know that this race is not given to the swift but to those that endure. We won't allow the times nor the demonic forces to cause us to be anxious and run ahead of you. We will be still and see the salvation of the Lord. We will serve you, Lord, by the strength that you supply. For when we are weak, we will say we are strong. When it looks like there is no way, we will say when you open a door no man can close it. When it looks like all hope is gone, we will trust in you, our Blessed Hope! When it looks like we have lost everything, like David, we will encourage ourselves and recover all because you have promised to restore everything that the canker worm has eaten. Every battle that is formed against us is in vain for it won't prosper. Thank you for victory that is guaranteed when we trust you, Lord, in Jesus' Name!

AUGUST 23

Psalm 125:1

They that trust in the LORD shall be as mount Zion, which cannot be removed, but abideth for ever.

DECREE FOR TODAY: We decree that the favor of God is upon us! We are unstoppable!

Father, in Jesus' Name, thank you for every trial, every test, every obstacle, and everything that you have allowed to touch our lives for we know that every one of them had to be approved by you before the enemy could touch us as your people. Grateful that you trusts us enough to Stand in spite of, and it is all because of your mercy! Thank you for choosing us, making us royal, special people that cannot be defeated in you! You are not a man that you should lie, but if you spoke it, it shall come to pass. And though it tarry, we will wait for it! We will wait patiently for you, Lord, and in our patience, we will possess our souls. We won't fear. We won't go ahead of you. You promised to direct our paths, if we acknowledge you in all of our ways. Thank you for the power that you have placed in our tongues. We speak life today to every dead situation around us. We shall live and not die, in Jesus' Name, we thank you Lord!

AUGUST 24

John 14:27

Peace I leave with you, my peace I give unto you: not as the world giveth, give I unto you. Let not your heart be troubled, neither let it be afraid.

DECREE FOR TODAY: We decree that we will cease from anger. We will answer with a soft answer!

Father, in Jesus' Name, thank you – you've done it again – woke us up and we still have access to the creator of the world! Glory to God! We still have your promises in view, and we still have breath in our bodies. Only a God can do this! Thank you, Lord! And though all things may not be in our view, we know that they are already in place. Your thoughts towards us are good and not evil and to give us an expected end! Thank you. Victory is already ours! Peace that surpasses all understanding is ours. Healing belongs to us, because of the stripes you took at Calvary! Thank you, God! We are calling those things that are not into being. We are speaking to our mountains today and they got to move! Every high place must come down. Every valley will be filled! All of your promises are yea and amen! In Jesus' Name, we thank you!

AUGUST 25

Genesis 1:1

In the beginning God created the heaven and the earth.

DECREE FOR TODAY: We decree that better is the ending of a thing than the beginning! We will wait on God!

Father, in Jesus' Name, great is thy faithfulness towards us, Lord! It is a day of thanksgiving. Thank you for making us to be just what you desire us to be, to look like, and to live in this planet. You designed us for your glory! So, no matter how we feel about ourselves, you put the pattern together – help us to be grateful and thankful for your design. Help us to love ourselves as you created us, for we are here to glorify you and not others. Thank you for giving us your Word. It is food for our souls, directions for our daily lives, and a guide to greater knowledge of you! Thank you that the earth is still standing today, still in place. It is all by your power, Lord. Thank you for living in us - the greatest power in the earth. Thank you for the angels that you have supplied to encamp round about us, though most times we forget they are there! Thank you for giving us the right to call those things that are not as though they be! We bless you Lord. We honor you as King of Kings and Lord of Lords, in Jesus' Name!

AUGUST 26

<u>Psalm 145:21</u>

My mouth shall speak the praise of the LORD: and let all flesh bless his holy name for ever and ever.

DECREE FOR TODAY: We decree that we will humble ourselves before Almighty God! We will not be disturbed by demonic influences!

Father, in Jesus' Name, thank you that we can stay rooted and built up in you. You've given us what we need to be stablished in the faith. We won't be spoiled by philosophy and vain deceit. We are complete in you Lord and we can do all things through you because of the strength that you supply. We won't be anxious. You know the way that we take, Lord. We won't fear what is happening around us. We won't be dismayed! You are our God and you promised to strengthen us, yea you will help us and uphold us with your right hand of righteousness! When we pass through the waters and the rivers – the tough times of this life, you won't let them drown us. When our situations are heated as fire, you won't let us be burned. Thank you God! We have your promise that when the righteous cry and you hear, you will deliver them out of all their troubles. Thank you Lord, in Jesus' Name!

AUGUST 27

<u>1John 4:8</u>

He that loveth not knoweth not God; for God is love.

DECREE FOR TODAY: We decree that we will not turn to the right nor to the left. We will stand and see the salvation of the Lord!

Father, in Jesus' Name, thank you for blessing us to see another moment in the land of the living. We don't take it lightly. Thank you for the power of the Holy Ghost that enables us to weather every storm and come out stronger in you. We know that nothing can happen in our lives without your permission. We know that you are watching our goings and comings daily. Thank you for mercy and grace following us. We are grateful for your caring for us, Lord. No human could care for us better than you. We give you glory. We honor your presence in the earth. We acknowledge your greatness as we look around your creation. We appreciate your daily provisions. Thank you, Lord, for hearing our cries when we call. In Jesus' Name, we thank you!

AUGUST 28

Jeremiah 33:3

Call unto me, and I will answer thee, and shew thee great and mighty things, which thou knowest not.

DECREE FOR TODAY: We decree that we are the head and not the tail! God said so!

Father, in Jesus' Name, thank you for this new day, a day of new beginnings, new things, new minds, new determinations, because we are determined to take our faith to another level in you. We are looking unto Jesus the author and finisher of our faith. We won't look to the left nor to the right. We will renew our minds, Lord, to think as you would have us to think. We yield our hearts and minds to you, to mold us spiritually so that we can stand strong in these evil days. We shall not be moved by things we hear or see! You promised to go before us. We will not fear anything; demons, people, things nor allow anything to have dominion over us! We will speak your Word for in it is life! Our faith is standing not in the wisdom of man but in the power of God! We know the just shall live by faith and it is impossible to please you without it! We shall live and not die! Glory to God. In Jesus' Name, we thank you Lord God!

AUGUST 29

Nahum 1:7

The Lord is good, a strong hold in the day of trouble; and He knoweth them that trust in Him.

DECREE FOR TODAY: We decree that this is not our battle! It belongs to the Lord!

Father, in Jesus' Name, thank you for peace today. You are not the author of confusion, but the God of peace! You always cause us to triumph in

Christ. You have already redeemed us from the hand of the enemy. Thank you Lord. You promised us that we would have sweet sleep. Thank you for the angels that camp round about us! Thank you for the Holy Ghost that helps us to tidy up things in our lives. We will examine ourselves. We will not be guilty of unforgiveness, bitterness, and resentment. We will not harbor anything in our hearts that is not like you. We will not be bound by doubt, unbelief and negativity. We know you are our strength and shield. You are nigh unto all that are of a broken heart. You are the healer of the broken hearts and you bind up those wounds. Thank you Lord! We will practice to be quiet for in quietness and in confidence shall be our strength. Thank you Lord, in Jesus' Name!

AUGUST 30

Romans 8:28

And we know that all things work together for good to them that love God, to them who are the called according to his purpose.

DECREE FOR TODAY: We decree that we will not be bitter. We will forgive, even as Christ forgave us!

Father, in Jesus' Name, we pray a special prayer today for those in the military and their families, Lord, that you will cover them under the blood. Dispatch angels to watch over those on the battlefield. Cover their hearts Lord so that they will draw strength from you. Let them not be afraid of the pestilence by day nor the arrow by night. You are our defense, Lord. No weapon formed against us shall prosper. Bless those that have children, Lord. Fill up every space in the lives of all reading this prayer. You are our Comforter. We are trusting you to give them the desires of their hearts according to your divine will. Our faith is in you, Lord, and in you there is no failure. We hold on to it with confidence that every struggle and every trial shall pass. We thank you for it, in Jesus' Name!

AUGUST 31

Ecclesiastes 3:1

To every thing there is a season, and a time to every purpose under the heaven.

DECREE FOR TODAY: We decree that we will not let our hearts be troubled. We believe God!

Father, in Jesus' Name, we bless you. We praise you. We lift your name on high. In spite of our circumstances, we will worship you. We will remember you during our daily activities. We won't fail to acknowledge you, Lord. You see all things. You hear all things. Nothing is hidden from you. Thank you for your protection. You promised that no good thing would you withhold from those that walk upright. You said, the just shall live by faith. It is in you that we live, we move, and we have our being. Help us to daily be Christ-like. Help us to respond with a soft answer, for it turneth away wrath. Thank you for every trial, for they make us better. We give you glory, in Jesus' Name!

SEPTEMBER 1

Psalm 23:1
The LORD is my shepherd; I shall not want.

DECREE FOR TODAY: We decree that we are fully persuaded that God is able to do what he said he would do!

Father, in the Name of Jesus we come with a grateful heart today that you have allowed us an opportunity to spend eternity with you. God we thank you for our trials, though some may be difficult, some we don't understand, some seem like mountains too high to climb. But, Lord, we know that nothing is too hard for you! We have this assurance in us that all things are working together for our good! Thank you for the peace of God that surpasses all understanding! We are not afraid of Satan, Lord. You have already defeated him! We are not afraid of tomorrow, for you have said take no thought about it. We have the faith that you have given us that will help us to stand up, face anything, and go forward even when we don't see our way! And, Lord, for those shedding tears today, there is hope for you said weeping may endure for a night, but JOY will come in the morning! Glory to God! Hallelujah! Thank you for living inside of us, in Jesus' Name!

SEPTEMBER 2

1 Corinthians 4:5
Therefore judge nothing before the time, until the Lord come, who both will bring to light the hidden things of darkness, and will make manifest the counsels of the hearts: and then shall every man have praise of God.

DECREE FOR TODAY: We decree that God is our strength and our help in the time of trouble!

Father, in Jesus' Name, it is a day of thanksgiving to honor you and give you some glory. Thank you for the air you daily supply without fail so that we can breathe. You give life and breath and all things. Thank you! You deliver us from the snare of the fowler and from the noisome pestilences that we face day after day. You don't hide your ear from our cries. Nothing is too hard for you! Thank you, God, for your love. You raise those that are bowed down. You strengthen our hands when they are weak! You bring us out of distresses when the troubles of our hearts are enlarged. You deliver us out of all of our afflictions. You uphold all that fall. Glory to God! The waters – rivers – trials of this life are not allowed to overflow us and bury us in our sorrows for you never fail to lift us up out of our pits! Hallelujah! We love and adore you Lord and praise you, in Jesus' Name!

SEPTEMBER 3

Jeremiah 29:11
For I know the thoughts that I think toward you, saith the LORD, thoughts of peace, and not of evil, to give you an expected end.

DECREE FOR TODAY: We decree that God is our healer and our deliverer. Nothing is too hard for him!

Father, in the Name of Jesus, we don't always know what to pray for but, Lord, you said the Spirit makes intercession for us. So Lord we come boldly to your throne because you have given us that opportunity, and we bring with us the needs we sense for your people. Lord, sick bodies need healing. Many need places of shelter, food, and clothing. And, we know that you are the provider. We stand in the gap for those that seem not to have strength left because of the cares of this life. But, God, we know that you are without a doubt the lifter of all bowed down heads. You give strength to those that are faint. You supply grace when we've gone beyond your word. You offer forgiveness to all of us that will ask for it. Send a refreshing to your people's spirits, Lord. There is no failure in you. We need minds renewed. We know your power! We thank you for change, for we believe it will happen, in Jesus' Name!

SEPTEMBER 4

2 Samuel 23:5
Yet he hath made with me an everlasting covenant.

DECREE FOR TODAY: We decree that God is the lifter of the bowed-down head! He will strengthen us, yea he will help us!

Father, in Jesus' Name, thank you for birthing us into your spiritual kingdom! Glory to God! And, Lord, like little children standing before their parents with their requests, our hearts and spirits are standing in line, waiting for your answers. We won't grow weary to the point that we quit. Oh no, Lord God! You've given us mercy and grace to follow us all of our days to lift us, and to call to our remembrance what you have already done in the past! Thank you for giving us faith, for by faith we stand! And Lord for some, the battles seem to be overwhelming but you have already told us that the battles are not ours; they belong to you. You've given us a sign that you will answer; your Word is our sign that you won't forsake us. Help us to hide it in our hearts so that when the fiery darts come, Lord, they won't destroy our hearts. Glory to God. Bless us today, Lord, that no matter what we face, we know that though our afflictions may be many, you WILL deliver us out of them all. We thank you for it, in Jesus' Name!

SEPTEMBER 5

John 11:35
Jesus wept.

DECREE FOR TODAY: We decree that God's grace is sufficient for us!

Father, in the Name of Jesus, thank you for preserving the souls of the saints and delivering us out of the hand of the wicked. You are our confidence! Your word declares that in quietness and in confidence shall be our strength! Glory to God! The desire of the righteous shall be granted! Your word is settled in heaven! Thank you Lord that the enemy cannot change your word. Your promises to us are yea and amen! You are a refuge for those that are oppressed and a refuge in the times of trouble. We will use our shield of faith and quench every fiery dart of the enemy! Our needs will be met. You promised that if we seek first the kingdom of God and your righteousness, all these things will be added unto us! We believe it, Lord. We receive it. In spite of the winds and in spite of the storms, we won't doubt you, Lord. We will trust in your Word and thank you for it, in Jesus' Name!

SEPTEMBER 6

Job 27:6

My righteousness I hold fast, and will not let it go: my heart shall not reproach me so long as I live.

DECREE FOR TODAY: We decree that no storm has lasted forever! We will use our faith to weather every storm! This too shall pass!

Father, in Jesus' Name, thank you for the special privileges you have given to your people. You have blessed us to know the mysteries of your kingdom. Hallelujah! Thank you for permitting the kingdom of God to be within us. What a blessing. We were sinners, without God, hopeless and caught up in the evil things of this world. But, we thank you for sending grace! Glory to God! Thank you for allowing grace to continue to follow us all the days of our lives. Thank you for access to this great grace through faith wherein we stand and rejoice in hope of the glory of God! Thank you for protection. Thank you for healing. Thank you for making known to us the riches of your glory! We rest in you, Lord! In Jesus' Name, we thank you!

SEPTEMBER 7

Psalm 117:1 & 2

O praise the LORD, all ye nations: praise him, all ye people. For his merciful kindness is great toward us: and the truth of the LORD endureth for ever. Praise ye the LORD.

DECREE FOR TODAY: We decree that we will praise God in spite of our circumstances!

Father, in Jesus' Name, thank you for giving us the opportunity to pray. Your word declares that if we call upon you, you will answer. You will be with us in trouble. Even before we call, you will answer. We ask for your divine will, in your answers, as you know what is best for us Lord. We won't be anxious, but in everything we will give thanks and let our requests be made known to you, Lord. When we pray, we will believe you, and your word says that if we believe that we have received it, it will be ours. Hallelujah! We are going to pray without ceasing. Thank you for the Spirit that helps us in our weakness. We don't always know what to pray for, but thank you that the Spirit intercedes with groanings that we don't understand, but, thank you, Lord! In Jesus' Name!

SEPTEMBER 8

Matthew 7:2

For with what judgment ye judge, ye shall be judged: and with what measure ye mete, it shall be measured to you again.

DECREE FOR TODAY: We decree that God's mercy and grace are following us! Nothing can harm us!

Father, in Jesus' Name, we are waiting on you, Lord. Many have requests before you. We will wait, because we know that you shall renew our strength. You will mount us up on wings of eagles. We won't grow weary; we will run, we will walk, and we shall not faint! We will be strong; our hearts will take courage, as we wait for you. We will trust in you with all of our hearts. We won't lean unto our own understanding. And, Lord, we will acknowledge you in all of our ways. We know you will make our paths straight and direct us. You are good to those that wait for you and seek your face. Thank you for the open door to come into your presence. In Jesus' Name, we thank you, Lord!

SEPTEMBER 9

Acts 2:38

Repent, and be baptized every one of you in the name of Jesus Christ for the remission of sins, and ye shall receive the gift of the Holy Ghost.

DECREE FOR TODAY: We decree that God's plans for us are good and not evil and to give us an expected end!

Father, in Jesus' Name, you have made us to sit together in heavenly places! Glory to God! And, Lord, some today are not feeling on the mountain. Truth be told Lord, none of us are always on the mountain. So we ask that you will lift the bowed down heads today. You have given us the garment of praise for the spirit of heaviness. And for those that seem to be losing hope because of their circumstances, we pray that joy will overtake them. Let your past miracles surface in the minds of your people. What would we have done, Lord, if you had forsaken us in times past! Oh glory! You have been faithful. Never late! Hallelujah! We rebuke the demonic spirit of haste! We command it to leave your people now! You have our lives all planned out according to your divine design. Help us to wait on the Lord and be of a good courage. For in due time, we will reap, if we faint not! Thank you for this assurance, in Jesus' Name!

SEPTEMBER 10

Isaiah 55:11

So shall my word be that goeth forth out of my mouth: it shall not return unto me void, but it shall accomplish that which I please, and it shall prosper in the thing whereto I sent it.

DECREE FOR TODAY: We decree that we will praise God in the midst of chaos. He has given us a garment of praise for the spirit of heaviness!

Father, in Jesus' Name, we are grateful for this moment in time that you have so freely given us, and one that we won't see again; we will take advantage of it and give you some glory! We praise you, because you live, we can live also. Hallelujah! We will shake off everything that comes to hinder us. We will go forward! We will not be deceived by the enemy. We have your Word as our guide! We know that with you, Lord, all things are possible. We will not lean to our own understanding! We will not fear. We will stand like the Psalmist and though the earth be moved and the mountains be carried into the sea, we will stand in you Lord! The God of Jacob is with us! In the midst of our troubles and trials, you stand tall, Lord, to deliver us out of all of our afflictions! Glory to God! Thank you for being the potter that keeps us together even during those times when the enemy would want to sift us as wheat! You have prayed for us. Thank you Lord, in Jesus' Name!

SEPTEMBER 11

Psalm 37:5

Commit thy way unto the LORD; trust also in him; and he shall bring it to pass.

DECREE FOR TODAY: We decree that though we walk through the waters, God will not let them overflow us; through the fire, he won't allow us to burned!

Father, in Jesus' Name, it is a day of thanksgiving to honor you for sacrificing your blood for us. Oh God where would we be without you! Thank you for suffering, enduring excruciating pain, taking it without saying anything! Thank you Jesus! Thank you for looking beyond our faults and seeing our needs! We give you glory! Thank you for grace and mercy that is following us day by day. Thank you for supplying every need according to your riches in glory by Christ Jesus. Thank you for the angels that you have given us that keep watch over us. Oh God, how we thank you that you have given us power to protect our souls from the enemy. We are grateful for the ability to shake off those things that try to attach themselves to us and destroy our hope! Grateful that greater is the God inside of us than the devil in the world. We bless you and thank you Lord, in Jesus' Name!

SEPTEMBER 12

Isaiah 54:17

No weapon that is formed against thee shall prosper; and every tongue that shall rise against thee in judgment thou shalt condemn. This is the heritage of the servants of the LORD, and their righteousness is of me, saith the LORD.

DECREE FOR TODAY: Though we walk through the shadows of death, we will fear no evil. God's rod and staff will comfort us!

Father, in Jesus' Name, thank you for all you have done for us and that you are planning to do. Your plans towards us are good and not evil and to give us an expected end! We believe it. Sometimes, we are not on the mountain top and we are not feeling victorious. But, we stand on your word that says, we walk by faith and not by sight. Sometimes, we feel that our night is too long. But, you said weeping may endure for a night, but joy is coming in the morning! When we feel we can't, your word says we CAN do all things through Christ that strengthens us! We know that every mountain shall be made low, and every crooked place shall be made straight. We won't faint, Lord! We will pray until change comes! We will pray until our faith is built to face our obstacles head on, knowing that the battles are not ours. They belong to you Lord. Thank you for being mighty in our lives! You are the Lord, the Lord strong and mighty! Thank you Lord, in Jesus' Name!

SEPTEMBER 13

Isaiah 59:19

So shall they fear the name of the LORD from the west, and his glory from the rising of the sun. When the enemy shall come in like a flood, the Spirit of the LORD shall lift up a standard against him.

DECREE FOR TODAY: We decree that God has given us power to walk on the devil's head!

Father, in Jesus' Name, we thank you for the ability to have faith! It will see us through the dark places. And Lord some are facing difficult situations today. Giant-like situations are causing some to fear. But, God, we want to take on David's spirit when he was preparing to face Goliath, he said let no man's heart fail because of Goliath. You said, let not your heart be troubled! We will rest in you, Lord. We will use the sword of the Spirit which is the word of God to defeat everything that rises up against us! Your Word is like a hammer that breaketh the rock in pieces! Healing is ours! Provision is ours! Peace is ours! Deliverance is ours! Glory to our God! It's in your Word, Lord, and we receive it, in Jesus' Name! We will walk and think like we are victorious, because of the greatness of the God that is in us! You are our Rock! Thank you Lord, in Jesus' Name!

SEPTEMBER 14

Deuteronomy 6:4-5

Hear, O Israel: The Lord our God is one Lord: And thou shalt love the Lord thy God with all thine heart, and with all thy soul, and with thy might.

DECREE FOR TODAY: We decree that the joy of the Lord is our strength!

Father, in Jesus' Name, it is a day of thanksgiving! We give you glory for the ability to feel your presence. Lord we are grateful that you have put a power within us that is undefeatable! Thank you, Jesus. Thank you for food, clothing and shelter. Thank you for the eyes you have given us to be able to read and see your creation. Thank you for opening our spiritual eyes so that we cannot be deceived! Thank you for peace that is available to us in the midst of the worst, most devastating situations. Yes, God! Thank you for knowing that nothing, absolutely nothing is too hard for you! And, Lord, though we are but the dust of the earth, thank you for building us so that nothing can separate us from your love! Nothing can disconnect us from you as long as we abide in you. Thank you, Jesus! God, we thank you for families today wherever they may be; thank you for covering them! We give you glory and thanks, in Jesus' Name!

SEPTEMBER 15

John 14:6

Jesus saith unto him, I am the way, the truth, and the life: no man cometh unto the Father, but by me.

DECREE FOR TODAY: We decree that tough it tarry, yet shall it come! We will wait on the Lord!

Father, in Jesus' Name, thank you for your awesome love for your people. We have all come short of your glory but you have not ceased to allow grace and mercy to continue to follow us. Thank you, Lord! You give power to the faint. You are our strength! We will wait on you Lord. We will be of a good courage because we have no doubt that you will strengthen our hearts! Thank you for the confidence you have put in us that helps us when having done all, to Stand! By faith, we will cross our Red Seas, by faith we will be still when we should and know that you are God and watch you work the miraculous in our lives! There is no failure in you Lord. You will turn our tears into joy! We'll let go of the mental battles for the battles are not ours, they belong to you Lord! Thank you for being the Master of our situations, in Jesus' Name, we thank you Lord!

SEPTEMBER 16

1 Peter 1:3

Blessed be the God and Father of our Lord Jesus Christ, which according to his abundant mercy hath begotten us again unto a lively hope by the resurrection of Jesus Christ from the dead.

DECREE FOR TODAY: We decree that in quietness and peace we will serve the Lord!

Father, in the Name of Jesus, thank you for arming us with the power of God that makes every demonic force subject to us! We will not be defeated. We will walk in our victory this day! We will speak to those circumstances and situations that are trying to overwhelm your people, make them doubtful and discouraged! We know there is nothing too hard for you. We are going to speak to our mountains in faith. We will call those things that are not as though they were. We won't fear nor be dismayed. You are our God! Yes, Lord! You will help us. You will strengthen us for this journey! You will uphold us! You will hear our cry. Glory to God! We will walk in our victory today, knowing that we are the King's children! We have the authority to speak to the devil, cast him out – out of our homes, out of our minds, and out of everything that is not like you! You will deliver our souls in peace from every battle that is against us! God, we thank you, in Jesus' Name!

SEPTEMBER 17

2 Corinthians 5:17

Therefore if any man be in Christ, he is a new creature: old things are passed away; behold, all things are become new.

DECREE FOR TODAY: We decree that the blessings of the Lord maketh rich and he addeth no sorrow with it!

Father, in Jesus' Name, you have redeemed us from the hands of the enemy, for that we say thank you! We thank you for bringing us to this moment. We don't take it lightly. We count every moment precious Lord! Lord we pray for every one that is sick in the body. Heal them according to your will. The Psalmist said, you sent your word and healed them and delivered them from their destruction. Someone is waiting, Lord. Do it again! Hallelujah! You are the same yesterday, today and forever! You have declared that many are the afflictions of the righteous, but the Lord delivereth them out of them ALL! Many are in a struggle in the mind, in finances, in broken relationships! God grant them miracles from these afflictions. You said, if we abide in you and your word abides in us, we can ask you anything and you will do it – according to your divine will we receive it. We thank you for it, Lord, in Jesus' Name!

SEPTEMBER 18

Philippians 3:13

Brothers, I do not consider myself yet to have taken hold of it. But one thing I do: Forgetting what is behind and straining toward what is ahead, I press on toward the goal to win the prize for which God has called me heavenward in Christ Jesus.

DECREE FOR TODAY: We decree that the Lord is our provider. He will supply all of our needs according to his riches in glory by Christ Jesus!

Father, in Jesus' Name, thank you for strength to go forward. When we are feeling too weak to see that you have already made the way, you make us strong. Hallelujah! You are our refuge. You promised to bless the righteous and wrap favor around us as a shield! Thank you for the angels that camp round about us wherever we are. You daily deliver us out of the hand of the wicked. Thank you for the times when you cover us when our eyes are not focused on the now! Thank you for preserving us when we go out and come in. We will not be afraid of sudden fear, nor the devil. You are our confidence. Glory to God! When the enemy comes in against us like a flood, you promised that the spirit of the Lord will lift up a standard against him; for that we say thank you Lord. We will rest in you, Lord, for you have promised that whoever hearkeneth unto you shall dwell safely and be quiet from the fear of evil. In Jesus' Name, we thank you!

SEPTEMBER 19

2 Corinthians 5:6,7

Therefore we are always confident, knowing that, whilst we are at home in the body, we are absent from the Lord (For we walk by faith, not by sight).

DECREE FOR TODAY: We decree that we will put our trust in God. We will not fear what man can do unto us!

Father, in Jesus' Name, we come boldly to your throne today, and we are grateful that you have granted us that permission! Thank you, Lord! It is an honor to have your presence in our lives. Thank you for choosing us and bringing us out of a wicked world. Glory to God! We love you. We do not deserve the favor you have given us, and your mercy and grace towards us is unmeasurable! Thank you for erasing our past. Thank you for casting our sins into the sea of forgetfulness. Now, Lord, we ask that you will help us to renew our minds daily, to renew our attitudes, and our speech so that we will have a soft answer for every man. God, let our hands find good to do. Help us not to be busy bodies in other men's matters. Renew a right spirit within us, Lord. We are striving to be strong in you and armed against our adversaries, with the Word of God. Thank you Lord, in Jesus' Name!

SEPTEMBER 20

Psalm 27:1

The LORD is my light and my salvation; whom shall I fear? the LORD is the strength of my life; of whom shall I be afraid?

DECREE FOR TODAY: We decree that God has forgiven us of our sins! We will not allow satanic forces to bring up our past!

Father, in Jesus' Name, thank you that you are the vine and we are the branches. We have an assurance that as long as we stay attached to you and abide in you and your words abide in us, we shall ask what we will and it shall be done, according to your divine will. Thank you, Lord! You chose us and ordained us that we should bring forth fruit. We are to be your witnesses. Help us to walk this earth like the King's kids, in assurance that everywhere our feet shall tread shall be victory for us. Hallelujah! Victory on the street, victory on the job, victory in the home! It's ours according to your divine will! So what shall we say unto these things, Lord, if God be for us, who, WHO can be against us! Glory to God! Lord, we thank you for arming us with the power of the Holy Ghost – it covers us, covers our minds, covers our thoughts, and covers our actions! Glory to God! Father, we thank you, in Jesus' Name!

SEPTEMBER 21

Matthew 5:8
Blessed are the pure in heart: for they shall see God.

DECREE FOR TODAY: We decree that our eyes have been enlightened. The devil can't fool us!

Father, in Jesus' Name, thank that mercy watched over us during the night and grace woke us up today! Glory to God! We bless you! We praise you! We love you, Lord! Oh how we adore you! We are going to go about our daily goings in strength, in hope, and in assurance that whatever we encounter today, you have already conquered it. Every demon we meet is already defeated. Every foe on the job, in the home, or wherever is already brought down! Glory to God! You said our blessings will overtake us, run us down! You said we will be blessed in field and in the city! Glory to God! Violence in the cities won't stop our blessings! Unexpected happenings won't stop our blessings! We got the word! And everything is going down but your word, God. Hallelujah! In Jesus' Name, we thank you!

SEPTEMBER 22

1 John 4:20
If a man say, I love God, and hateth his brother, he is a liar. For he that loveth not his brother whom he hath seen, how can he love God whom he hath not seen?

DECREE FOR TODAY: We decree that we will not be intimidated by anyone – not on the job, in the home, nowhere! The peace of God is ours!

Father, in Jesus' Name, thank you for mercy and grace! Lord we have all come short, but your mercy has kept us afloat. Your love has lifted us above our circumstances and trials and made us to sit together in heavenly places. Thank you for the anointing that breaks every yoke. We bless your Name for it is excellent in all the earth. Thank you for our eyes today Lord to see both naturally and spiritually. My God, how awesome you are, Lord. Our two little eyes allow us to naturally see the Universe and spiritually see beyond the natural and behind the flesh face, so that we are not deceived. Hallelujah! Thank you for our feet today, Lord, that help us to travel great distances without thinking about them. Our fingers, Lord, that can be taught how to move separately. You thought about all of this before creating us! My My, God, we thank you, in Jesus' Name!

SEPTEMBER 23

<u>Romans 6:23</u>

For the wages of sin is death, but the gift of God is eternal life through Jesus Christ our Lord.

DECREE FOR TODAY: We decree that whatever we ask God in Jesus' Name, it shall be done according to his divine will. It shall be!

Father, in the Name of Jesus thank you for the Blood of Jesus! Oh how grateful we are for being covered under the blood. Help us to realize the power in your Name, Jesus! We will stand strong as good soldiers, enduring the trials of this life. You said to count them all joy! Glory to God. Your word says leap for Joy! You are the strength of our life! Hallelujah! You are our provider, our healer, and our deliverer. Everything we need is in you! Thank you for the power of the Holy Ghost that helps us to walk right, talk right, and obey your word. In spite of our short-comings, you have never forsaken us, never left us. Thank you for the gift of faith that keeps us Standing! Having done all, we can still STAND! Bless the children, Lord. Let your angels go with them on the school buses, in the school rooms. Bless the teachers. We rebuke the bullies aggravating the children and adults on the jobs. The blood of Jesus is against that bullying demon! Thank you Lord, in, Jesus' Name!

SEPTEMBER 24

<u>John 1:12</u>

But as many as received Him, to them gave He power to become the sons of God, even to them that believe on His name.

DECREE FOR TODAY: We decree that God has given us power over our thoughts! We will not lean unto our own understanding!

Father, in Jesus' Name, we rejoice in our salvation. Thank you for the opportunity to spend eternity with you, Lord. Help us to wear this life as a loose garment for it is as a vapor that soon passes away. Thank you for your love and peace that surpasses all understanding. Forgive us of our sins, Lord, those that we willingly do and those that are not our intent. Bless your people not to be anxious, discouraged or depressed. We rebuke those spirits, in the Name of Jesus. You are still all power regardless of what the world looks like. When you speak, everything has to obey. Bless the minds of your people. Help us to look to you in all things for your Name is a strong tower. The righteous runneth into it and is safe. Make the devil behave today, Lord, on the job, in the home, wherever! Thank you Lord, in Jesus' Name!

SEPTEMBER 25

Psalm 118:8
It is better to trust in the LORD than to put confidence in man.

DECREE FOR TODAY: We decree that Jesus is Lord! There is no other lord over us! Tell the devil God said so!

Father, in Jesus' Name, it is a day of thanksgiving. Thank you for the air that we breathe. Thank you for purifying it. Thank you for giving man the knowledge to purify water so that we can drink and not thirst to death. Oh God we thank you! Thank you for the veins in our bodies that you use to keep the blood flowing. Should it shut down, life would be no more. Oh God we thank you for giving us blood. Thank you for shedding your Blood so that we can live eternally. Man's shedding of human blood would be to no avail for us, but yours was perfect, matchless and powerful enough to bring life through the shedding. Oh how excellent you are, Lord! Thank you for a brand new day and for defeating every demon that will be traveling our paths today! Thank you for the power to conquer even our thoughts, Lord, in Jesus' Name!

SEPTEMBER 26

Philippians 3:10
That I may know him, and the power of his resurrection, and the fellowship of his sufferings, being made conformable unto his death.

DECREE FOR TODAY: We decree that we will not be discouraged, we will not be depressed, and we will not give up! God has better!

Father, in Jesus' Name, thank you for this great Salvation plan for us. We love you Lord. Bless our children. Keep them safe on the street, on the school buses, in the classrooms. Bless the teachers. Cover them Lord! We plead the blood of Jesus against every plan of the adversary. We command the devil to get out of here! We are standing on the Rock! The power of the Holy Ghost is greater than any demon walking the earth and traveling the air. We rebuke you Satan. Get out of the minds of God's people. You are a liar, Satan. God said you are the Father, of lies. God said we are more than conquerors! We believe Him! In Jesus' Name, we thank you Lord!

SEPTEMBER 27

Nahum 1:7

The Lord is good, a strong hold in the day of trouble; and He knoweth them that trust in Him.

DECREE: We decree that we will lay aside every weight that is weighing us down and will not carry unnecessary things in our minds.

Father, in the Name of Jesus, we say yes to your will, whatever it is, Lord we say yes! Many are the afflictions of the righteous but the Lord delivereth them out of them ALL! We say Hallelujah! You told us to count it all joy when troubles come our way! Dry every tear drop today, Lord. You said weeping may endure for a night buy JOY comes in the morning. Turn nights into morning now, Lord, for your people that are waiting. We know you are never late. Victory is already ours for you have made us more than conquerors. Help us to lay down our weapons of the flesh and begin to war in the spirit through prayer. Glory to God! We thank you for prayer Lord, in Jesus' Name!

SEPTEMBER 28

Philippians 1:6

Being confident of this very thing, that he which hath begun a good work in you will perform it until the day of Jesus Christ.
DECREE FOR TODAY: We decree that our trials and troubles are working for our good. God said so!

Father, in the Name of Jesus, today is a day of thanksgiving. We thank you for life and for the Holy Ghost, the power that lives within! Glory to God!

Thank you for the strength to endure hardness as good soldiers. Thank you for provision, shelter, food and all of the things that we take for granted! Great is thy faithfulness, oh Lord! We thank you that you have kept us in our right minds, looking unto Jesus the author and finisher of our faith! Thank you for this day and whatever it brings because your word says it is working for our good! Glory to God! Thank you Lord for being unchangeable, a God that we can depend on without doubting our victory! Hallelujah! In Jesus' Name, we thank you Lord!

SEPTEMBER 29

Jeremiah 33:3

Call unto me, and I will answer thee, and shew thee great and mighty things, which thou knowest not.

DECREE FOR TODAY: We decree that the blood of Jesus has set us free from condemnation. We will not allow man to condemn us!

Father, in Jesus' Name, thank you for your promises. All of them are yea and amen! We are calling those things that are not as though they be! We are speaking to our mountains and they must come down! Every valley will be filled! Thank you that no weapon formed against us shall prosper. We claim being the head and not the tail according to your word. We know that you hear us, Lord, when we pray according to your will. Bless those that are feeling heavy. You have given us a garment of praise for the spirit of heaviness. We rebuke every foul spirit attacking your people. Discouragement, depression, and frustration got to go! The blood of Jesus is against you Satan. We speak peace and life in disastrous situations, in Jesus' Name!

SEPTEMBER 30

Psalm 37:4

Delight thyself also in the LORD; and he shall give thee the desires of thine heart.

DECREE FOR TODAY: We decree that this is the day the Lord hath made! We will not allow evil forces to take our joy!

Father, in the Name of Jesus we pray for those that are incarcerated, those unjustly and those justified. We ask for mercy Lord. Open doors, Lord! We pray for those incarcerated in the mind. Lord, you are the answer to all things! We won't be bound by the demons of hell. We will stand, having done all. You are in our midst. We won't be moved! Lord you are able to do far above what we think or ask according to the power that works in us! We take authority over the evil forces of hell trying to discourage your people. Greater is he that is in us than he that is in the world. We know it! We believe it! We thank you, Lord, in Jesus' Name!

OCTOBER 1

<u>Psalms 27:1</u>

The LORD is my light and my salvation; whom shall I fear? the LORD is the strength of my life; of whom shall I be afraid?

DECREE FOR TODAY: We decree that God is going to shut the mouths of the gainsayers! Walk in victory!

Father, in Jesus' Name, thank you for all spiritual blessings inside of us that you have put in heavenly places in Christ that lives within. Thank you for choosing us before the foundation of the world. Through your blood we have redemption from sin! Glory to God! Thank you for not remembering our sins, our faults, and our short-comings! Increase our faith, Lord. Take us to new levels in you, do a new thing, new revelations, and new experiences. Bless our children. Cover them under the blood day and night as they go to and fro. We thank you for it, in Jesus' Name!

OCTOBER 2

<u>Revelation 22:21</u>

The grace of our Lord Jesus Christ be with you all. Amen.

DECREE FOR TODAY: We decree that we will not harm anyone with the words of our mouths!

Father, in Jesus' Name, it is a day of thanksgiving! Giving you glory that as we slept during the night you kept us from the hands of the enemy. Thank you for the angels that camp round about us! Thank you that we can feel your presence, Lord. Oh God, what would we do without your presence in this wicked world? Hallelujah! Thank you for the Word of God that speaks to the core of our pains, our sickness, our provisions, our thoughts, and our minds! Glory to God! Thank you for a memory that we can go and return just by thinking. My Lord, I thank you, God! We give you praise for who you are in our lives, in Jesus' Name!

OCTOBER 3

Romans 12:1

Therefore I urge you, brethren, by the mercies of God, to present your bodies a living and holy sacrifice, acceptable to God, which is your spiritual service of worship.

DECREE FOR TODAY: We decree that we will face whatever comes our way today with confidence that God's got it!

Father, in Jesus' Name, thank you for being a due time God! You are never late! We praise you for every shut door, every trial, and every hard and difficult place, everything that has come our way. You have permitted it and therefore we say thank you for allowing us to go through! If you didn't think we could handle it, you would not have permitted it. Glory to God! Hallelujah to Jesus! Thank you for your promises that are all yea and amen! Thank you that your thoughts are higher than our thoughts and your ways are not like our ways! Bless us with renewed minds daily! Thank you for the joy of the Lord that is our strength! We praise you for peace that surpasses all understanding! Peace in the midst of turmoil! Glory to God! Peace in the midst of chaos in the home, on the job, in the schools, and on the street. Wherever! God we walk in our victory today and we thank you for it, in Jesus' Name!

OCTOBER 4

Hebrews 10:24-25

Let us think of ways to motivate one another to acts of love and good works.

DECREE FOR TODAY: We decree that we will dwell in the secret place of the Most High! God's got us covered!

Father, in Jesus' Name, thank you for the blessings you have bestowed upon your people. You woke us up this morning. What a miracle! We rejoice in our sufferings. We know that suffering results in endurance, which builds our character and that gives us hope. Our souls wait for you.

Thank you for your compassion and mercy. You are steadfast. You are awesome, Lord. We will look to you, the God of our salvation. We will take our stand and look to see what you will say to us, Lord. You are our light and our salvation. You are the stronghold of our lives. We will not be afraid of anyone. Even if an army encamps against us, our hearts will not fear. We will be confident and hope in you! In the day of trouble, you will hide us in your shelter. In Jesus' Name, we thank you!

OCTOBER 5

Ephesians 4:29

Don't use foul or abusive language. Let everything you say be good and helpful, so that your words will be an encouragement to those who hear them.

DECREE FOR TODAY: We decree that it is well; in spite of how it looks!

Father, in Jesus' Name, thank you for giving us strength and power over the news Lord! We are going to hide ourselves in the Word of God. We will not fear. You have not given us that spirit, but one of power, love and a sound mind. We will not be disturbed by hearsay! We will not allow our minds to wander into doubt! For greater is he that is within us than he that is in the world! We speak victory, we speak healing, and we speak provision into the lives of your people. For we are a royal priesthood, a chosen generation a peculiar people, resting in the peace of God! We thank you for it, in Jesus' Name!

OCTOBER 6

Colossians 3:16

Let the word of Christ dwell in you richly in all wisdom!

DECREE FOR TODAY: We decree that when the enemy comes in like a flood, the Spirit of the Lord is going to lift up a standard against him! Tell the devil God said so!

Father, in Jesus' Name, it is a day of thanksgiving – not asking for anything in this prayer. Thank you for our circumstances for they are your will for us. Glory! Thank you for your love that is everlasting. Thank you for healings, provisions, and doors opened! Thank you for the kingdom of God within us that cannot be shaken! Oh God, we bless you today! Thank you for this privilege to know you and your power that can change us, our surroundings and everything that touches us is subject to you. Thank you God, in Jesus' Name!

OCTOBER 7

Ecclesiastes 4:9

Two people are better off than one, for they can help each other succeed. If one person falls, the other can reach out and help.

DECREE FOR TODAY: We will take on Job's spirit today! Though God slay us, yet will we trust him!

Father, in Jesus' Name, thank you for being so amazing! You are the light of our lives, God! We bless you, Lord! We ask that you will cover the children around the world. The enemy desires to sift them as wheat, but God we stand on your word! No weapon formed against us shall prosper. What touches the children touches us. The enemy is bound. Drug dealers that are coming against the children, we bind them up under the blood of Jesus. Violence is bound today. Alcohol is bound. Let the angels assist the children. Remove fear from them Lord. We thank you for it, in Jesus' Name!

OCTOBER 8

Romans 15:7

Accept one another, then, just as Christ accepted you, in order to bring praise to God.

DECREE FOR TODAY: We decree that vengeance belongs to the Lord! He will repay!

Father, in Jesus' Name, thank you for your love that is beyond explanation! Thank you for fighting our battles. They all belong to you, Lord. Help us not to interfere. Thank you for being our blessed Hope, for hope deferred makes the heart sick. We won't allow our hearts to be troubled! We refuse to bow to the trickery of the enemy for any reason. We have your promise to bring down every stronghold through your spirit. We won't be deceived on the job, in the home, wherever! We are not ignorant of the enemy's devices. Thank you for arming us with your discernment. Thank you for the blood flowing through our veins freely. Thank you that when we woke up this morning our memory was still intact. Glory to God. In Jesus' Name, we thank you for a victorious day!

OCTOBER 9

<u>Proverbs 27:9</u>

The heartfelt counsel of a friend is as sweet as perfume and incense.

DECREE FOR TODAY: We decree that we will not worry! He that planteth the ear, shall he not hear. He that planteth the eye, shall he not see!

Father, in Jesus' Name, we are grateful for the blood that you shed at Calvary. It has already defeated every demonic force. It has already spoken for sick bodies to be delivered, the oppressed to be delivered, the discouraged to be encouraged, and the depressed to be made glad! Glory to God! It's all through the blood of Jesus! God thank you for making us victorious in every situation! You are our Rock! Our Joy! Our Peace! Our Provider! Our Protector. You are everything we need. And Lord, things that are not present, you have promised to supply. We are going to use our faith to cross our Red seas, to speak to our mountains, to Stand, having done all! In Jesus' Name, we thank you Lord!

OCTOBER 10

<u>1 Thessalonians 5:14</u>

And we urge you, brothers and sisters, warn those who are idle and disruptive, encourage the disheartened, help the weak, be patient with everyone.

DECREE FOR TODAY: We decree that we will hold our peace, even from speaking good if necessary! It's the Lord's battle!

Father, in Jesus' Name, thank you for encouraging us day by day! You continue to make sure the sun rise so that we are not constantly walking around in a dark world. Glory to God! We will continue to trust you, Lord for you are our strength! You have ordained peace for us! You declared that blessed is the man that maketh the Lord his trust! Thank you Jesus! There are those in the Hall of Faith in your Word, help us to be living members of the Hall of Faith in the earth! Help us to stretch our faith when it seems like there is no hope. For you are our Hope, our blessed Redeemer! Who can stop you from performing your word for us! There is none Lord – no weapon! Hallelujah! Thank you Lord, in Jesus' Name!

OCTOBER 11

<u>Provers 27:17</u>

As iron sharpens iron, So a man sharpens the countenance of his friend.

DECREE FOR TODAY: We decree that the just shall live by faith!

Father, in Jesus' Name, thank you for this moment whatever it is holding, whether it be joy, pain, hurt, disappointment, whatever! You said give thanks for all things are working together for our good. We are not asking for anything today but it's a day of thanksgiving! Thank you Lord for getting rid of our old ways and our old thoughts that were not like you and renewing our minds! Glory to God! Thank for throwing our sins into the sea of forgetfulness! Thank you Jesus for destroying bitterness for it makes the body sick. Glory to God! Thank you for our mountains! We know they are coming down. Thank you for our enemies. We will watch you spread a table before us in their presence. Thank you for mercy and goodness following us and leading us in the right paths God. Glory to your Name Lord in Jesus' Name, we thank you!

OCTOBER 12

<u>2 Corinthians 1:4</u>

Who comforts us in all our troubles, so that we can comfort those in any trouble with the comfort we ourselves have received from God.

DECREE FOR TODAY: We decree that we will fear no evil. The Lord is with us!

Father, in Jesus' Name, thank you for being bigger than the world, bigger than our faults, bigger than our difficult situations! Glory to God! We honor you, Lord. We rebuke the spirit of heaviness in the land. You have given us a garment of praise to defeat it! We will sing unto the Lord! We will lift up the bowed down heads. We won't faint, Lord. Thank you for giving us memory. Oh Lord where would the world be without memory in us! Thank you for the ability to feel your presence. My God, where would we be, Lord, if you pulled your presence from the earth! Lord Jesus! Thank you that we can talk to you. We can communicate with you regardless of what level we are on and you make us feel royal! Glory to God! Hallelujah! Thank you Lord, in Jesus' Name!

OCTOBER 13

Romans 15:1

We who are strong in faith should help the weak with their weaknesses, and not please only ourselves.

DECREE FOR TODAY: We decree that we are blessed when we go out and blessed when we come in, regardless of what we see! It's God's word! We will speak it!

Father, in Jesus' Name, you are our Rock! Our souls wait upon you Lord! We know Lord God that all power in earth and heaven belongs to you! Our souls can rest in you and you alone! Our hope is not in the things of this world but in you Lord. Your loving kindness is better than life. You have been our help. You have kept us when we were persecuted on the job, on the street, in the home, wherever, we were not forsaken! Troubled on every side, but you didn't allow us to become distressed! Thank you, Lord God! Though a host should encamp against us, we will not fear! No weapon! Hallelujah No weapon regardless of its nature formed against us shall prosper. We receive it, Lord, in Jesus' Name!

OCTOBER 14

Matthew 7:14

Because strait is the gate, and narrow is the way, which leadeth unto life, and few there be that find it.

DECREE FOR TODAY: We decree that we will hold fast. We will not be led by ungodly counsel.

Father, in Jesus' Name, thank you for the air that we breathe. We will go through this life with total dependence on you. We know that the sufferings of this present time are in no way worth comparing with the glory that you will reveal in us. We await your return. We will be still and wait patiently for you to answer our prayers. We will not fret ourselves over others that prosper or those that carry out evil things. You loved us so much that you gave your Son, so that whoever believes in him should not perish. We believe, Lord. We will not be like the five foolish virgins that took no oil with them and when the bridegroom came, they were left behind. The door was shut. We will be ready for your return, Lord. We will keep this precious anointing that you have given us. We thank you, in Jesus' Name!

OCTOBER 15

Isaiah 35:4

Say to those who are fearful-hearted, Be strong, do not fear! Behold, your God will come with vengeance, With the recompense of God; He will come and save you.

DECREE FOR TODAY: We decree that we will not be a stumbling block in the way of saints, sinners, friends or family!

Father, in Jesus' Name, thank you for this moment in time that is precious, help us to cherish it for it will soon be gone. We are going to trust you, Lord and not lean to our own understanding! We won't fear, we won't be dismayed for you are our God! Our strong tower! Our strength! We will not be shaken. We will cast all of our anxieties upon you for you care for us Lord! Walk in the hospitals Lord, in prisons, in homes, let your anointing arrest ever demon in our paths. Strengthen our faith, Lord. Let the weak say I'm strong. In the midst of all of the chaos going on in this world, Lord, we know that you still reign. Glory to God. We thank you Lord, in Jesus' Name!

OCTOBER 16

Romans 14:19

Let us therefore follow after the things which make for peace, and things wherewith one may edify another.

DECREE FOR TODAY: We decree that we will not be jealous, envious, troublemakers, or deceitful.

Father, in Jesus' Name, thank you for the open door to your throne! Wow, Lord, what a privilege you have given us to speak to the God of the Universe. You are awesome. Through the storms, through the pains, through the hard times, you have remained faithful. You've never been late. You've never failed! Glory to God! You are yet helping your people to stand in the midst of a world filled with chaos. Your word says, in the world we will have tribulations but you encouraged us to take heart, because you have overcome the world! Nothing in this world can harm us if you be for us. Thank you Lord, in Jesus' Name!

OCTOBER 17

<u>Romans 15:4</u>

For everything that was written in the past was written to teach us, so that through endurance and the encouragement of the Scriptures we might have hope.

DECREE FOR TODAY: We decree that we will endure hardness as a good soldier in the home, on the street, on the job, wherever! God is our defense!

Farther, in Jesus' Name, we thank you for coming into the earth. You have experienced all that we go through. And, Lord, for some, they sometimes feel as no one understands their problems. But Lord you know! You walked this earth. And though it was in the plan for our salvation, you were betrayed by one you called and you gave power to do miraculous things. And, Judas, even being a devil, you treated him the same. Yes, you do know Lord! We thank you for being touched by our infirmities, in Jesus' Name!

OCTOBER 18

<u>Galatians 6:2</u>

Share each other's burdens, and in this way obey the law of Christ.

DECREE FOR TODAY: We decree that we will do good, especially to those of the household of faith!

Father, in Jesus' Name, our souls wait in silence for you. Our salvation comes from you, Lord. We are sure of this one thing that you began this good work in us, and you will bring it to completion when you return. We lift our eyes unto you. As the eyes of a maidservant looks to the hands of her mistress, so our eyes look to you Lord God. Have mercy upon us. We will walk in your ways and obey your word, so that we may prosper in all that we do. We will do everything in your Name, Jesus! We will meditate on your word. We will not repay evil. Vengeance belongs to you, Lord. Our help comes from you. In Jesus' Name, we thank you!

OCTOBER 19

Ephesians 4:31-32

Let all bitterness, and wrath, and anger, and clamour, and evil speaking, be put away from you, with all malice: And be ye kind one to another, tenderhearted, forgiving one another, even as God for Christ's sake hath forgiven you.

DECREE FOR TODAY: We decree that we will cease from anger.

Father, in Jesus' Name, thank you for Calvary. Your blood is still as fresh today as it was the day you shed it on Calvary. The blood covers, it protects us. Glory to God! Because of it we can speak those things that are not as though they were. We can walk in victory, and meet every challenge without fear! During times of disappointments and uncertainties, the blood still works! Bless every home here today, Lord. You are able to do exceedingly abundantly above all that we ask or think. Give us a double portion of anointing! Thank you for the power to stand down the demons of hell, Lord. We speak peace in the minds of your people, and we thank you for it right now, in Jesus' Name!

OCTOBER 20

Ephesians 4:25-26

Wherefore putting away lying, speak every man truth with his neighbour: for we are members one of another. Be ye angry, and sin not: let not the sun go down upon your wrath.

DECREE FOR TODAY: We decree that we will bless the Lord! We will lift our hands and tell him Thank You!

Father, in Jesus' Name, thank you for this moment in time to give you a Hallelujah! Thank you, Jesus! We are stepping out in faith this day, knowing that you are directing our steps, Lord! Knowing that you have grace and mercy following us every day gives us an assurance that all is well! Glory to God! Lord, we have all come short but we know that you have a blood bank that covers our sins and the spirit of forgiveness that allows us to go forward! We leave yesterday behind, Lord. We leave the last hour, the last minute behind, and we are forgetting those things that are behind us as we press towards the mark for the prize of the high calling of God in Christ Jesus! Glory to God! Cover the children in these wicked days, Lord. We pray for peace in their lives! We speak it, we declare it to be so in the Name of Jesus, and we thank you, Lord!

OCTOBER 21

James 1:19

Understand this, my dear brothers and sisters: You must all be quick to listen, slow to speak, and slow to get angry.

DECREE FOR TODAY: We decree that this day we will be strong in the Lord and in the power of his might! We will not be nervous about anything in the house, on the street, on the job, wherever! Jesus never panicked, nor will we! God is bigger than that!

Father, in Jesus' Name, thank you for being our shepherd, our guide, our protection through dangers and things unseen. God, we give you glory for being our stronghold. We don't have to be afraid of anything. Nothing! You will exalt us above our enemies and spread a table before us in their presence. Oh Lord how great is your goodness that you have stored up for those that reverence you! You have given us wisdom so that we are not ignorant of the devil's devices so he cannot deceive us. Thank you Lord! You have commanded the oceans and the seas not to go beyond their borders, so that they won't drown us. Thank you, Lord God, for watching over us; your word declares that you behold all of our goings! Glory to God! Hallelujah! In Jesus' Name!

OCTOBER 22

James 4:11

Speak not evil one of another, brethren. He that speaketh evil of his brother, and judgeth his brother, speaketh evil of the law, and judgeth the law: but if thou judge the law, thou art not a doer of the law, but a judge.

DECREE FOR TODAY: We decree that we will look unto the hills from whence cometh our help; our help cometh from the Lord!

Father, in Jesus' Name, thank you for mercy and your precious lovingkindness. We will delight ourselves in you. We will humble ourselves and pray and turn from our wicked ways so that you can heal the land Lord. Thank you for speaking to your people. We will stand, having done all. We will walk uprightly. We wait for you, Lord. We will not run ahead of you. Thank you for protecting us from dangers that we did not see. Thank you for binding the hands of the enemy that came against us and continuing to keep the enemy at bay. We bless you for provisions, Lord. We thank you that we can lift our hands without doubting your word but standing on your promises. We pray for the children. Cover them under your blood. We bind the bullying spirit that has plans to come against the children of your people. Tie them up, Lord, and help them to see you in the midst of their evil doings. Deliver them. Set them free from the powers of darkness. In Jesus' Name, we thank you Lord!

OCTOBER 23

<u>James 5:16</u>

Confess your faults one to another, and pray one for another, that ye may be healed. The effectual fervent prayer of a righteous man availeth much.

DECREE FOR TODAY: I decree that I will guard my ways so that I may not sin with my tongue.

Father, in Jesus' Name, thank you for a new day! Oh how blessed we are to wake up in the land of the living. You have given us another opportunity to ensure that we are in right standing with you and ready to stand before you Lord. For, every knee must bow and every tongue must confess that Jesus is Lord. Thank you for choosing us, counting us worthy to suffer for your sake, arming us with the power of the Holy Ghost to go forth in this chaotic world. Thank you for the power that is available to anyone that asks. We bless you for establishing us, sitting us in heavenly places in Christ Jesus, miraculously creating each of us as unique individuals to you and watching our daily goings. Oh what power you have Lord. Among the billions of people in the earth, you hear each one when they call. Thank you Lord. We give you all the gory, in Jesus' Name!

OCTOBER 24

<u>Psalm 77:11</u>

I will <u>remember</u> the deeds of the Lord; yes, I will remember your wonders of old.

DECREE FOR TODAY: We decree that we will not go back! We will go forward in the strength of the Lord!

Father, in Jesus' Name, great is thy faithfulness unto us oh Lord. We will be strong in the power of your might. We will not worry because of evildoers, and Lord, we will not be envious toward those that do us wrong.

We will trust you. We will rely upon you. Our confidence is in you Lord. We will delight ourselves in you. We stand on your word. You promised if we delight ourselves in you that you will give us the desires of our hearts. We know that it will be within your divine will, as our desires will become your desires for our lives. Keep us under the blood of Jesus. Keep our minds as we wait patiently for you. In Jesus' Name, we thank you!

OCTOBER 25

Romans 15:5

May the God who gives endurance and encouragement give you a spirit of unity among yourselves as you follow Christ Jesus.

DECREE FOR TODAY: We decree that the sufferings of this present time are not worthy to be compared with the glory which shall be revealed in us.

Father, in Jesus' Name, we give you all the glory and honor. Thank you for lifting up the bowed down heads. Thank you for keeping the wicked at bay. Your word says you laugh at the wicked one that oppresses the righteous. We will be still and see the salvation of the Lord. We will not look at others' prosperity and be envious. Your word declares that better is the little of the righteous, those that strive to be in your divine will, than all of the riches of the wicked. You have promised to supply all of our needs according to your riches in glory by Chris Jesus. We believe it. We receive it, in Jesus' Name!

OCTOBER 26

Philippians 4:8

Finally, brethren, whatsoever things are true, whatsoever things are honest, whatsoever things are just, whatsoever things are pure, whatsoever things are lovely, whatsoever things are of good report; if there be any virtue, and if there be any praise, think on these things.

DECREE FOR TODAY: If God be for us, who can be against us and stand successfully? Absolutely no one!

Father, in Jesus' Name, thank you for directing our paths. You have declared that the steps of a good man are directed by you Lord. You establish our comings and our goings. You are the Great I AM. You are the one that sustains us day after day. No good thing will you withhold from those that walk uprightly. That is your word, Lord, and we thank you! You have never abandoned your people that walk uprightly. We desire to dwell in that secret place in you, Lord. Thank you for that opportunity. Thank you for the peace that surpasses all understanding. In Jesus' Name, we thank you!

OCTOBER 27

Psalm 19:14

May the words of my mouth and the meditation of my heart be pleasing in your sight, O LORD, my Rock and my Redeemer.

DECREE FOR TODAY: We decree that things present, nor things to come shall be able to separate us from the love of God!

Father, in Jesus' Name, thank you for the salvation plan that you put in place before the foundation of the world. Thank you for choosing us. Thank you for forgiving us of all of our sins and throwing them into the sea of forgetfulness. You are our refuge. You are our stronghold in the time of trouble! You are always there to rescue us in times of need. Bless your Name, Lord! Nothing can separate us from your love – no friend, no family, nothing! We know that we are more than conquerors through Christ. The battles are not ours; they belong to you, Lord. We will let go, and let God! In Jesus' Name, we thank you!

OCTOBER 28

Hebrews 3:13

But encourage one another daily, as long as it is called Today, so that none of you may be hardened by sin's deceitfulness.

DECREE FOR TODAY: We decree that we will love our neighbors and work no ill towards them.

Father, in Jesus' Name, thank you for protecting us and keeping the plagues away from our dwellings and keeping us from destruction. Thank you for putting your love upon us. When we call upon you, we know you will answer according to your divine will. How great you are. How great are your works in the earth and in our lives. How great are your thoughts towards us. Your plans towards us are good and not evil and to give us an expected end. We receive the promise and we thank you for it, in Jesus' Name!

OCTOBER 29

<u>1 Thessalonians 5:18</u>

In every thing give thanks: for this is the will of God in Christ Jesus concerning you.

DECREE FOR TODAY: We decree that we will walk in honesty, and not in strife and envying!

Father in Jesus' Name, we will declare your wondrous works in the earth. You are greatly to be praised. We worship you in the beauty of holiness. You reign. The world shall not be moved because you have established it. We will not be concerned about the happenings in the world. Our focus is on striving toward the mark for the prize of the high calling of God in Christ. We wait for the Blessed Hope! In Jesus' Name, we thank you, Lord!

OCTOBER 30

<u>Psalm 136:1</u>

Give thanks to the Lord, for he is good! His faithful love endures forever.

DECREE FOR TODAY: We decree that we will not judge our brother. For we shall all stand before the judgment seat of Christ.

Father, in Jesus' Name, thank you for giving us an opportunity to spend eternity with you. Thank you for giving us the Holy Ghost to prepare us for the hereafter, where there will be no more dying, no more crying, no more pain! Glory to God! We rejoice in knowing that there is a crown laid up for those that endure. Thank you for strengthening your people for this journey. In Jesus' Name, we thank you!

OCTOBER 31

<u>Psalm 9:1</u>

I will praise You, O LORD, with my whole heart; I will tell of all Your marvelous works.

DECREE FOR TODAY: We decree that we will be wise and not cause our good to be evil spoken of.

Father, in Jesus' Name, thank you for the price you paid for us at Calvary. We will glorify you in our daily lives. Whatever we do, we will do it all to your glory. We will honor you with the firstfruits. We love you with all of our hearts and souls with all of our might, Lord. We will be vessels for honorable use and set apart as holy and useful to you, Lord, being ready for whatever you have called us to do. We are your temple. Thank you for the Spirit that dwells in us as we accept you as our Lord. Help us to keep the vows that we pledge and to do according to all that comes out of our mouths in honor of you. We choose to serve you until the day of our redemption. In Jesus' Name, we thank you, Lord!

NOVEMBER 1

<u>Psalm 69:30</u>

I will praise the name of God with a song; I will magnify him with thanksgiving.

DECREE FOR TODAY: We decree that we will follow after peace and things that edify others!

Father, in Jesus' Name, thank you for your provisions. We will share. We will not be stingy. We will not oppress the poor, for that insults you, Lord. We will be generous to the needy. We will not store up an abundance, while our neighbors go in need. We will be helpers of one another. You weigh our spirits. We will commit our works unto you to establish our plans. You have made everything for a purpose. Make us to know your ways, Lord. Teach us your paths. We won't be anxious, but in everything we will by prayer, while giving you thanks, make our requests known unto you. Thank you for the peace of God that surpasses all understanding. We will guard our hearts and our minds in you. Thank you Lord, in Jesus' Name!

NOVEMBER 2

Psalm 103:2

Bless the LORD, O my soul, and forget none of His benefits; Who pardons all your iniquities, Who heals all your diseases, Who redeems your life from the pit.

DECREE FOR TODAY: We decree that our faith will NOT stand in the wisdom of men, but in the power of God!

Father, in Jesus' Name, blessed are those that trust in you and make you their hope. We refuse to be caught up in the cares of this life. We will not be anxious. Having done all, we will stand! We will be still! We will wait on you, Lord. We will acknowledge you in all of our ways, knowing that you will direct our paths. Thank you, Lord, for giving us a mind. We can meditate on your word and hide it in our hearts so that we won't sin against you. We can read your word and be renewed in the Spirit and receive hope and assurance that all things are working for our good. We give you glory, in Jesus' Name!

NOVEMBER 3

Psalm 92:1

It is a good thing to give thanks unto the LORD, and to sing praises unto thy name, o most high.

DECREE FOR TODAY: We decree that we will not walk as carnal men – envying and full of strife! NO! We will build ourselves up in God so that we can eat strong meat of the Word of God!

Father, in Jesus' Name, thank you for blessings us, choosing us, and trusting us to be your witnesses in the earth. Help us to always let our speech be with grace and seasoned with salt. Help us to stand perfect and completely in the will of God. Lord in all that we do in word or deed, help us to do it heartily as to the Lord, and not unto men. In Jesus' Name, we thank you!

NOVEMBER 4

1 Chronicles 16:8

Give thanks unto the LORD, call upon his name, make known his deeds among the people

DECREE FOR TODAY: We decree that we are the temple of God and we will not defile it!

Father, in Jesus' Name, it is a new day, a new hour, a new moment in time given to us to praise you, to honor you, and to worship you. Thank you Lord! We pray for those that are feeling crushed today and pressed beyond measure. We are going to count it all joy. When we are tried and suffering for your sakes, your strength will enable us to go through. We know, through your word, that we are more than conquerors through Christ. In Jesus' Name, we thank you!

NOVEMBER 5

Psalm 145:7

The fame of your goodness spreads across the country; your righteousness is on everyone's lips.

DECREE FOR TODAY: We decree that we will not be puffed up! We will humble ourselves under the hand of the Almighty – even on the job!

Father, in Jesus' Name, we are blessed! Blessed in the city! Blessed in the field! Blessed when we go out and come in! Your word declares it to be so. We pray for those that have need of a renewal of the mind. Comfort their hearts, Lord. Strengthen their faith. Restore! Help us to be steadfast in you. All of your promises are yea and amen! We believe it! We claim it! We declare it over ourselves and our families. You are not a man that you should lie. Thank you for the promises, Lord. By faith, we receive them in Jesus' Name!

NOVEMBER 6

Psalm 26:7

That I may proclaim with the voice of thanksgiving, and tell of all Your wondrous works.

DECREE FOR TODAY: We decree that we will not use our liberty in Christ to become a stumblingblock to those that are weak.

Father, in Jesus' Name, thank you for grace and mercy! Help us to stay rooted and built up in you and stablished in the faith, Lord. We are leaning on you and not unto our own understanding. Our hope is in you. We surrender ourselves to you totally in order that you, through your death on the cross, will present us holy and unblameable in your sight. We stand! Having done all, we stand! We rebuke the powers of darkness. We thank you for the authority you have given us to walk on the devil's head. Grateful to you Lord! In Jesus' Name, we thank you!

NOVEMBER 7

Psalm 35:18

I will give You thanks in the great assembly; I will praise You among many people.

DECREE FOR TODAY: **We decree that we will run this race well and not let anyone or anything hinder us!**

Father, in Jesus' Name, we submit ourselves to you in reverence of you, your Name, your power, your authority and your might! We love you, Jesus! Wash us with your word so that you can present us unto yourself a glorious church, not having spot or wrinkle, holy and without blemish. We will, through your Spirit, walk worthy of our vocation, wherewith you have called us. Thank you for your grace. Grant us according to your riches to be strengthened with might by your Spirit in our inner man. Bless us, Lord, to remain faithful. In Jesus' Name, we thank you!

NOVEMBER 8

Psalm 50:23

Whoever offers the sacrifice of thanksgiving glorifies me; And to him that orders his way aright will I show the salvation of God.

DECREE FOR TODAY: **We decree that we will be led by the Spirit!**

Father in Jesus' Name, we bless you for another day in the land of the living. Help us to guard our mouths so that we won't sin against you with our tongues. Help us to appreciate the days you have given us in this earth. Our confidence is in you. So many times, Lord, we have waited patiently for you and you heard our cries. You answered. Thank you, Lord! You have brought us up out of horrible pits and places of destruction. Only you! Only you could have rescued us. We are grateful! Your wonders are too numerous to count. Your thoughts towards us are good and to give us an expected end. We thank you! Thank you for your compassion, your tender mercy and your lovingkindness towards us, in Jesus' Name!

NOVEMBER 9

<u>Psalm 31:19</u>

Oh, how great is Your goodness, Which You have laid up for those who fear You, Which You have prepared for those who trust in You, In the presence of the sons of men!

DECREE FOR TODAY: We decree that that we will not be tossed to and fro, and carried about with every wind of doctrine, by the sleight of men.

Father, in Jesus' Name, thank you for peace in the midst of a troubled, and corrupt world of uncertainty. You have not lost your power and your presence makes us victorious over every challenge, every demonic activity and every thought that is not like you. Glory to God! Thank you that your thoughts are not like our thoughts and your ways are not like our ways. Thank you for the renewing of our minds! Trouble is in the land but you told us let not our hearts be troubled! Strengthen our faith, Lord! Elevate the minds of your people to weather every storm. You warned us about perilous times, Lord. They are here, but you are still the same. Our shield. Our battle-axe! Our deliverer! Our provider! Our strength in times of faint! Glory to God! In Jesus' Name, we thank you!

NOVEMBER 10

<u>Philippians 4:6-7</u>

Do not be anxious about anything, but in every situation, by prayer and petition, with thanksgiving, present your requests to God.

DECREE FOR TODAY: We decree that we will walk in love, as Christ loves!

Father, in Jesus' Name, thank you for the power of the Holy Ghost! Gory to God! We are going to take back everything the devil has stolen from us! And, Lord, we are going to do it by standing in your Word! Standing by faith on your promises! We won't raise our hands, but we will trust you by [illegible] for you are our battle-axe. You will restore everything that the canker worm has eaten. Those that have lost joy, we stand in the gap for them, Lord, that it will be restored, peace of mind, broken hearts, broken marriages, unsettled spirits! We claim the victory Lord! We won't take down in our minds, but we will renew them every day! The mind is the battlefield! We are going to keep it stayed on you Lord, for in doing that, you have promised us perfect peace. Glory to God we thank you Lord, in Jesus' Name!

NOVEMBER 11

James 5:13

Is anyone among you suffering? Let him pray. Is anyone cheerful? Let him sing praise.

DECREE FOR TODAY: We decree that we will have no fellowship with the unfruitful works of darkness. We will walk in the light!

Father, in Jesus' Name, we thank you for filling your people with the knowledge of your will in wisdom and spiritual understanding. Help us Lord to walk worthy of you and to be pleasing in your sight, and to be fruitful in every good work. Help us not to do evil works, Lord. Bless us to increase in the knowledge of you. Strengthen us Lord according to your glorious power. Help us to be patient, to go through, to be longsuffering, and not short-patient. Thank you for joy and when we don't have it, you said leap for joy! Thank you for forgiveness of our many sins. Thank you for cleaning us up and making us royal, peculiar people and chosen! Glory to God! From the mud to chosen! From the streets to Chosen! From adulterers to Chosen! Thank you Jesus! What a mighty God you are, Lord, and we thank you for grace in Jesus' Name!

NOVEMBER 12

Psalm 97:12

Rejoice in the LORD, ye righteous; and give thanks at the remembrance of his holiness.

DECREE FOR TODAY: We decree that we will redeem the time, because the days are evil! The Lord is coming soon!

Father, in Jesus' Name, thank you! We bless you, Lord. Thank you for knowing that we can have the confidence in you that if we ask you anything according to your will, you hear us. And, Lord, if we know that you hear us, your word declares that whatsoever we ask, we know that we have the petitions that we desire of you. Thank you God! Help us to line up our desires with your desires for us. Glory to God! Then we know without a doubt that we have them. Thank you for protection and assuring us that in all things, we are more than conquerors. You promised to preserve our going out and our coming in. Thank you God for being nigh unto us. Thank you for the angel that is camped round about us. You are our refuge! You are our help, Lord God, in Jesus' Name!

NOVEMBER 13

<u>Psalm 105: 1-2</u>

Oh, give thanks to the LORD! Call upon His name; Make known His deeds among the peoples! Sing to Him, sing psalms to Him; Talk of all His wondrous works!

DECREE FOR TODAY: We decree that we will be strong in the Lord and in the power of his might! Having done all, we will stand!

Father, in Jesus' Name, thank you for the hope we have in you. We will yet praise your Name! We rebuke the devil and every evil spirit that is speaking doubt, fear, discomfort, conflict, restlessness, and no peace! We rebuke the spirit of confusion and discouragement. Satan brings up the past, but you have already forgiven past sins. Glory to God! We crush the devil's head by the power of the Holy Ghost! Bless those that are afflicted today, Lord. Bring them out of distress. Overwhelmed in heart, but you said, let not your heart be troubled! We will speak your word, in confidence and assurance that no good thing will you withhold from them that walk uprightly. It is settled in heaven and in earth! God we thank you for who you are, in Jesus' Name!

NOVEMBER 14

<u>Psalm 27:1</u>

The Lord is my light and my salvation; whom shall I fear? The Lord is the stronghold of my life; of whom shall I be afraid?

DECREE FOR TODAY: We decree that we will not be terrified by our adversaries!

Father, in Jesus' Name, it is a day of thanksgiving; we are not asking for anything in this prayer. Lord, we are just giving you some glory! Praising you for the garment of praise! Honoring your Name for the power in it! Glory to God! Thanking you for making the sun and moon to still shine. What would we do without the sun shining, Lord! Oh glory to God! Thank you for protecting us during the night and making the devil behave! Thank you for water, Lord, so that we don't thirst to death! My My, God how you look out for us! Thank you for dispatching the angels to ward off the wicked demonic plans! My Lord, Jesus we thank you today for all things, in Jesus' Name!

NOVEMBER 15

Isaiah 41:10, 13

Don't be afraid, for I am with you. Don't be discouraged, for I am your God. I will strengthen you and help you.

DECREE FOR TODAY: We decree that we will forget those things that are behind us and reach forth for those things that are before us.

Father, in Jesus' Name, we come boldly to the throne thanking you for grace and mercy! And, Lord, many are broken-hearted; some are ready to abandon ship; some are holding on by splinters; some are saying, Lord, where are you? But this day, God, those who are building themselves up in prayer, stocking up on your word, stretching out on faith, some the size of a mustard seed, are reaching out and down to pull our brothers and sisters up the ladder of elevation in the Spirit so the fight of faith can become easier. Help us, Lord, to be strong in you and the power of your might! Your word says, the weakness of God is stronger than man's strength! Help our strength, Lord God, to go from strength to strength and we thank you, in Jesus' Name!

NOVEMBER 16

Psalm 9:10

Those who know your name trust in you, for you, O LORD, do not abandon those who search for you.

DECREE FOR TODAY: We decree that the peace of God which surpasses our understanding will keep our hearts and minds in this world of chaos!

Father, in Jesus' Name, thank you for making us victorious in every area of our lives! We give you glory! We are going to walk in confidence, in the power of the Holy Ghost that you have provided to live on the inside of us! We're going to be an example of you, Lord. You never looked defeated, you never expressed any kind of doubt, and you walked this earth as man full of power. Because you live inside of us, we can have that same walk, Lord! You knew you were going to Calvary and yet you went about doing good, healing the sick, delivering, and bringing hope! Glory to God! So, Lord, in the midst of the struggles that your people are facing today, we declare a victorious ending, for your thoughts towards us are good and not evil and to give us an expected end! Thank you Lord, in Jesus' Name!

NOVEMBER 16

Isaiah 2:22

Don't put your trust in mere humans. They are as frail as breath…

DECREE FOR TODAY: We decree that we will make every effort to be content in whatever state we are in until God changes it.

Father, in Jesus' Name, thank you for favor! Dry tears today, Lord. Help your people to remember that you have declared that weeping may endure for a night but joy is coming in the morning. Lord some spirits are overwhelmed within and like David, when his spirit was overwhelmed within, he looked on the right and there was no man to help, but, Lord God, he cried unto you. We are going to get up from where we are and go in your strength, Lord God! You are our Hightower, our deliverer, our shield in whom we trust! We are delivered, Lord God, on the job, in the home, wherever, even as you delivered David from the accusers and the lying spirits against him! No weapon that is formed against us shall prosper! That's your word Lord! Glory to God! We thank you today, in Jesus' Name!

NOVEMBER 17

Psalm 118:8

It is better to trust in the LORD than to put confidence in man.

DECREE FOR TODAY: We decree that God himself is going to present us unblameable in his sight, if we continue in the faith!

-

Father, in the Name of Jesus, thank you for the anointing that breaks every yoke! Let the spirit of prayer overtake us today, God. Heal sick bodies, in the Name of Jesus. We command the infirmities to leave right now. Every foul spirit is cursed. We command you to leave God's people alone. Poverty is cursed. Depression is cursed. Anxiety is cursed. We command you to go right now, in the Name of Jesus. You lying demon that is affecting marriages we plead the blood of Jesus against you. Infidelity is cursed! Hallelujah! We come against every power of darkness. Every bowed down head be lifted, in the Name of Jesus! Now Lord we go in the power of the Holy Ghost pulling down every strong hold and walking in our victory, knowing that every weapon formed against us shall not, glory to God, shall NOT prosper, in Jesus' Name we thank you!

NOVEMBER 18

Psalm 31:14-15

But as for me, I trust in You, O LORD; I say, You are my God. My times are in Your hand.

DECREE FOR TODAY: We decree that we will remain grounded and settled and not moved away from the great gospel of Jesus Christ! We won't be shaken by the trials of this life!

Father, in Jesus' Name, we thank you that you hear us when we call. And, Lord, today some are troubled and some go mourning even as David did. The desires are before you. The groanings are not hid from you. Our hope is in you. The enemy of the soul is strong, but you are greater than he is. For some Lord even as David, have felt that their tears have been their meat since they have been many. You are the restorer Lord God! We have this hope in us that weeping may endure for a night but joy cometh in the morning! You are our ROCK! Glory to God! Thank you! In Jesus' Name!

NOVEMBER 19

Psalm 20: 7-8

Some trust in chariots and some in horses, but we trust in the name of the LORD our God. They are brought to their knees and fall, but we rise up and stand firm.

DECREE FOR TODAY: We decree that we will not let any man spoil us through philosophy and vain deceit, after the tradition of men!

Father, in Jesus' Name, thank you for faith to take us through this journey of life. Lord some today don't want to go to work because of what they know is awaiting them. So, make the way, Lord. Give them favor. You speak, Lord. You own all of the jobs. What you say goes! Some of us are sick in body, but we declare by your word that healing belongs to us. You will deliver! God, some don't feel they have the means to make it, but you are our source! Glory to God! Do something supernatural for someone today, Lord. Our expectation is of you and we thank you, in Jesus' Name!

NOVEMBER 20

Psalm 27:1

The Lord is my light and my salvation; whom shall I fear? The Lord is the stronghold of my life; of whom shall I be afraid?

DECREE FOR TODAY: We decree that we will set our affections on things above, not on things of this earth.

Father, in Jesus' Name, thank you for this moment. A moment in time that we won't experience again, so help us to cherish it. Everything that we face today we will face in the Name of the Lord. Like David came against the giant Goliath in the Name of Lord, so shall we do, Lord God! Your Name is a strong tower and the righteous runneth into it and are safe! Glory to God! We are going to stand our tests, Lord, like Job, for we too shall come forth like pure gold! Lord, you blessed Job, in his lost you gave him twice as much as he lost. Do it for your people today. Restore what the canker worm has eaten. We claim it, we receive it, and we thank you, in Jesus' Name!

NOVEMBER 21

Jeremiah 32:27

Behold, I am the LORD, the God of all flesh; is anything too difficult for Me?

DECREE FOR TODAY: We decree that we will do nothing in vain glory; but we will humble ourselves and esteem others!

Father, in Jesus' Name, thank you for being our Rock! Thank you for making us steadfast, unmovable by every wind and doctrine. You are our Lord, our way maker, our provider, and our everything! God we bless you today for every trial, every hindrance, every obstacle, every stone thrown, and every evil word spoken against your people. Your word declares that all things are working together for the good for them that love you! Father we pray for those in nursing homes and hospitals today, Lord! We thank you for the nurses and the doctors and the aids. But Lord we need a change – we pray that you will turn things around – those being mistreated by mean aids, God. We need your help Lord. We bind up those demonic mean spirits, those hateful attitudes against the elderly. Satan we command you to go. Father, we pray that you will give those mean-spirited people a heart of compassion for the elderly. Do it Lord for your glory's sake and we thank you for it, in Jesus' Name!

NOVEMBER 22

Psalm 22:4

Our fathers trusted in thee: they trusted, and thou didst deliver them.

DECREE FOR TODAY: We decree that we will let patience have her perfect work in us!

Father, in Jesus' Name, thank you for this moment in time! We've been crucified with you, Lord, and we live in you Lord! And this life that we now live in the flesh, we live by faith through Christ! We know that you are the vine and we are the branches and if we abide in you, we can ask you anything according to your will and you will do it. Nothing is impossible for you! We will be strong in you, Lord! Bless those that are hanging on by a string – that's all they need to hang on. Rahab hung the scarlet thread in the window, and it brought salvation to her household, in the time of war. Our trust in you relieves us of fear and doubt. We are not afraid of the devil! Glory to God! The battle does not belong to us, it belongs to you, Lord. We win! We thank you for that, in Jesus' Name!

NOVEMBER 23

Isaiah 50:10

Who is among you that fears the LORD, That obeys the voice of His servant, That walks in darkness and has no light? Let him trust in the name of the LORD and rely on his God.

DECREE FOR TODAY: We decree that we will be doers of the word and not hearers only!

Father, in Jesus' Name, thank you for giving us common sense so that the devil cannot deceive us, and for giving us the spirit of discernment so that we are not tricked by the wicked spirits roaming the earth today. Glory to God! Help us, Lord, to hold on to the simplicity that is in Christ so that we don't present your word as though you are a hard task master, demanding rules and regulations, traditions that only bind our spirits. Help us not to present ourselves as high-minded and puffed up! We are saved by grace! You've set us free God. We thank you for the liberty that is in Christ Jesus! Your love is unmeasurable. Your tolerance and long-suffering with us goes beyond human understanding. Hallelujah! We'll walk in our freedom of spirit in the home, on the job, wherever! In Jesus' Name, we thank you!

NOVEMBER 24

Psalm 28:8

The LORD is the strength of his people, a fortress of salvation for his anointed one.

DECREE FOR TODAY: We decree that we will not have respect of persons; that is sin!

Father, in Jesus' Name, thank you for being God all by yourself. Glory to God! We rest in you, Lord! We are looking unto the hills from whence cometh our help. Our enemies are defeated, Lord. No weapon formed against us shall prosper. No great trial will overtake us. No discouraging news will cause us to be fearful. You planned our lives before we were born. We will count it all joy whatever today brings. You said, all things are working together for our good! We won't fret because of evil doers nor will we be envious of those that work iniquity. We are going to trust you and delight ourselves in you this day, Lord, in Jesus' Name, we thank you for your peace!

NOVEMBER 25

Psalm 31:24

Be strong, and let your heart take courage, all you who wait for the Lord!

DECREE FOR TODAY: We decree that the eyes of the Lord are upon the righteous and his ears are open unto their cries. He hears us!

Father, in Jesus' Name, thank you for these precious moments in time that we have never seen before. Help us to value the time you have given us here in the earth. Help us to daily prepare for your coming. Help us to speak the truth in love. Help us to guard our tongues so that we don't offend others. We give you glory! We bless your name for peace of mind. Thank you for making our bodies whole. You are our great physician. You are our healer. By your stripes we are healed. We will walk in the victory that you won at Calvary. No weapon formed against us shall prosper. We will wave our banners. We will leap over troops, regardless of what the enemy does or says. We are more than conquerors. Thank you for giving us this wonderful privilege to be called children of your kingdom. In Jesus' Name, we thank you!

NOVEMBER 26

<u>Psalm 46:1</u>

God is our refuge and strength, an ever-present help in trouble.

DECREE FOR TODAY: We decree that we will not fret ourselves because of evil doers! Vengeance belongs to God!

Father, in Jesus' Name, we give you glory for faith; a faith that can withstand anything that happens in this world. You have built us up with a spiritual resource that just keeps filling and refilling – giving strength, giving endurance in difficult circumstances! Glory to God! We won't allow our hearts to be troubled! We believe every word you have spoken, Lord! We are more than conquerors! Your grace is sufficient. Though we don't always see everything, our faith helps us to envision victory in all things! Whatsoever it is, we say thank you, Lord! Your thoughts are not like ours, and your plans are not like ours. Help us to live day by day, moment by moment totally depending on you. For in you Lord we live, we move and we have our being! Thank you Lord in Jesus' Name!

NOVEMBER 27

<u>Psalm 59:16</u>

But I will sing of your strength, in the morning I will sing of your love; for you are my fortress, my refuge in times of trouble.

DECREE FOR TODAY: We decree that we will abstain from the appearance of evil.

Father, in Jesus' Name, we lift up your Name on high! You are worthy to be praised. There is none like you in heaven or earth. Your name is to be glorified! Thank you for waking us up this morning. Thank you for the use of our limbs. We don't take it lightly Lord. We will meditate on your word day and night. Thank you for establishing us and sitting us in high places in Christ. Thank you for the whole armour of God that enables us to stand! Having done all, we will stand! We won't take down and we won't go back. We will move forward. We will be watchful! We will guard our tongues. We won't let our hearts be troubled. We will rest in you, Lord, knowing that you will order our steps according to your word. Thank you for directions! Thank you for helping us to stay in the narrow and right path. We bless your Name Lord and thank you, in Jesus' Name!

NOVEMBER 28

Psalm 105:4

Look to the LORD and his strength; seek his face always.

DECREE FOR TODAY: We decree that the Lord is faithful! He will establish us and keep us from evil!

Father, in the Name of Jesus, thank you for dying for us, Lord. The blood still works. Hallelujah! Today, Lord, some are troubled in spirit. That woman that is sitting at the table now with a cup of coffee wondering what next! Next is in your hands Lord, the God that holds the Universe together! You are able to do exceeding abundantly above all that we ask or think! We are troubled on every side yet not distressed. We are perplexed but not in despair Persecuted, but not forsaken. Cast down, but not destroyed! Glory! We faint not! We are looking at those things which are not seen but eternal. In Jesus' Name, we thank you!

NOVEMBER 29

2 Chronicles 16:9a

For the eyes of the LORD run to and fro throughout the whole earth, to show Himself strong on behalf of those whose heart is loyal to Him.

DECREE FOR TODAY: We decree that the Lord has not dwelt with us according to our sins nor rewarded us for our iniquities!

Father, in Jesus' Name, thank you for being mindful of us and blessing us. Your word declares the heavens are yours and the earth you have given to the children of men. Help us to be good stewards, Lord. We bless you. Thank you for inclining your ear unto us. You are our hiding place and our shield from all that would come against us. Our hope is in your word. We will speak your word in the home, on the job and wherever we go. Thank you for the word, Lord. It is like a hammer that breaketh the rock in pieces. It is our sword and defense. Everything is going down but your word. We stand on it and proclaim victory in every areas of our lives, because your word will stand against everything we encounter. In Jesus' Name, we thank you!

NOVEMBER 30

2 Timothy 4:17a

But the Lord stood at my side and gave me strength! so that through me the message might be fully proclaimed and all the Gentiles might hear it.

DECREE FOR TODAY: We decree that we will not fear. God is with us. Yea, He will strengthen us!

Father, in Jesus' Name, we thank you for your word declares that he that walketh uprightly walketh surely. Thank you that the mouth of the righteous is a well of life. Help us to be wells of life on a daily basis. Help us to speak good things, in spite of what we ae going through. The power of life and death is in the tongue. We know the hope of the righteous shall be gladness. In Jesus' Name, we thank you, Lord!

DECEMBER 1

Exodus 15:2

The LORD is my strength and my song; he has become my salvation. He is my God, and I will praise him, my father's God, and I will exalt him.

DECREE FOR TODAY: We decree that the Lord will perfect that which concerns us!

Father, in Jesus' Name, thank you for the power that worketh in us. Your word declares that the righteous shall never be moved! We will stand wherever we are. We will not fear man nor anything man plans; no weapon formed against us shall prosper. The righteous is delivered out of trouble and through knowledge shall the just be delivered. You have declared that a man of understanding holdeth his peace. We will be still and see the salvation of the Lord. Thank you, Lord, in Jesus' Name!

DECEMBER 2

<u>1 Chronicles 16:11</u>

Look to the LORD and his strength; seek his face always

DECREE FOR TODAY: We decree that God understands our thoughts!

Father, in Jesus' Name, thank you for grace. We pray for those that are going through and being attacked by demonic forces and lying spirits. Your word declares that a lying tongue is but for a moment. We will not fear what man can do against us. We will use our sword, which is the word of God, and defeat everything that exalted itself against us. Our hope is in you, Lord. Hope deferred makes the heart sick. We will look unto the hills from whence cometh our help. Our help cometh from the Lord. In Jesus' Name, we thank you!

DECEMBER 3

<u>1 Peter 4:11</u>

If anyone speaks, he should do it as one speaking the very words of God. If anyone serves, he should do it with the strength God provides!

DECREE FOR TODAY: We decree that God's thoughts towards us are precious! Who can harm us?

Father, in Jesus' Name, we bless you for giving us the Holy Ghost. Thank you for peace and joy. Thank you for delivering us from anger, because your word says, he that is soon angry dealeth foolishly. Help us to be witnesses for you. That is what you have called all of us to be. A true witness delivers souls. Help us to be about our calling, which is soul winning in our families, our communities, and in unlikeable places. Your Name is mighty, and it will deliver every sin-sick soul. We thank you for it, in Jesus' Name.

DECEMBER 4

<u>Nehemiah 1:10</u>

They are your servants and your people, whom you redeemed by your great strength and your mighty hand.

DECREE FOR TODAY: We decree that we are fearfully and wonderfully made by God!

Father, in Jesus' Name, thank you for righteousness. It exalteth a nation. Help us to remember the poor. Lord, you said if we oppress the poor, we oppress his Maker, that means you, Lord. Help us to speak softly. A soft answer turneth away wrath, but grievous words stir up anger. Your eyes are in every place beholding the good and the evil. We can't hide from you, Lord. Help us to deal honestly, with every man. In Jesus' Name, we thank you!

DECEMBER 5

<u>Nehemiah 8:10</u>

Do not grieve, for the joy of the LORD is your strength.

DECREE FOR TODAY: We decree that we will allow the Lord to set a watch before our mouths and keep the doors of our lips.

Father, in Jesus' Name, thank you for all of your provisions. Some of us are not where we think we should be, but your word says better is a little with the fear of the Lord than great treasures and trouble therewith. Help us, Lord, to remember to acknowledge you in all of our ways, for you will direct our paths. Your word declares that without counsel, purposes are disappointed. Before we counsel with man, we must counsel with you. Help us not to run ahead of you. You have already seen there, wherever there is. Help us not to be anxious but to wait patiently for you. In Jesus' Name, we thank you.

DECEMBER 6

1 Corinthians 1:25

For the foolishness of God is wiser than man's wisdom, and the weakness of God is stronger than man's strength.

DECREE FOR TODAY: We decree that will not allow our spirits to be overwhelmed by the cruelty of others.

Father, in Jesus' Name, thank you for this blessed day that you have allowed us to experience. Help us to lay aside the old man and walk in the newness of life. Help us to be humble in the home, in the workplace, and in the church. Help us not to be prideful, for pride goeth before destruction. Help us to deal wisely with one another, wherever we are. It is better to get wisdom than gold. That is your word! Help us not to be talebearers, for the words of a talebearer are as wounds and go down into the innermost parts of the belly. Help us not to wound others spiritually, but rather to love one another as you love us. In Jesus' Name, we thank you.

DECEMBER 7

Zechariah 4:6

Not by might nor by power but by my Spirit says the Lord God Almighty.

DECREE FOR TODAY: We decree that there is not a need that we have that God cannot supply!

Father, in Jesus' Name, thank you for your glory. We rest in your glory. Your presence is awesome, Lord. Your anointing refreshes us. Your compassion is unexplainable. Your mercy reaches beyond our comprehension. Thank you for dying for us. Thank you for climbing Golgotha's hill. Thank you for taking the beatings for us, which we deserved. But, your love! Oh God! What love! Thank you for seeing us delivered, while we were yet sinners. Thank you for going away to prepare a place for us, for where you are, we shall be, if we live right! Thank you Lord, in Jesus' Name!

DECEMBER 8

Romans 15:13

May the God of hope fill you with all joy and peace as you trust in him, so that you may overflow with hope by the power of the Holy Spirit.

DECREE FOR TODAY: We decree that God satisfies the desires of every living thing!

Father, in Jesus' Name, thank you for providing us a way of escape from the devourer that is like a roaring lion, roaming the earth, going to and fro seeking whom he can devour. We will watch! We will stand fast in the faith. We will be strong, continuing in prayer and with thanksgiving. We will hold fast and will not let any man take our crown. We know you are coming quickly! Help us to be ready, Lord. In Jesus' Name, we thank you!

DECEMBER 9

1 Corinthians 4:12

We toil, working with our own hands; when we are reviled, we bless; when we are persecuted, we endure!

DECREE FOR TODAY: We decree that he that keepeth his mouth keepeth his life: but he that openeth wide his lips shall have destruction. We will keep our mouths!

Father, in Jesus' Name, thank you for the gift of prayer. We bless you for this great tool that you have given us that brings peace to our souls. Prayer works! It is mighty! It reaches across the oceans and beneath the seas. It goes into hospitals and prisons. We can't physically see it, but we see the results of it. Glory to God! Help us to use our prayer time wisely. Help us to remember to worship you and give you glory! Thank you, Lord, that we woke up today on this side of eternity. You have given us another chance to get ready for your coming. We praise you, Lord. In Jesus' Name, we thank you!

DECEMBER 10

Matthew 5:12

Rejoice and be glad, for your reward in heaven is great; for in the same way they persecuted the prophets who were before you.

DECREE FOR TODAY: We decree that hope deferred maketh the heart sick: but when the desire cometh, it is a tree of life.

Father, in Jesus' Name, thank you for strengthening the body of Christ for this earthly journey. As we wait for you, our strength shall be renewed. We will mount up as eagles. We will run and won't grow weary. In our weakness, we will be made strong. We will walk and not faint. All of this because of you, Lord. We won't fear. We know you are with us. We won't be dismayed for you are our God! We know you will strengthen us and help us. Thank you for the joy. The joy of the Lord is our strength. In Jesus' Name, we thank you!

DECEMBER 11

1 Peter 4:13

But to the degree that you share the sufferings of Christ, keep on rejoicing, so that also at the revelation of His glory you may rejoice with exultation.

DECREE FOR TODAY: We decree that Good understanding giveth favour: but the way of transgressors is hard.

Father, in Jesus' Name, we come boldly before your throne today. We pray for those that feel as though they have no hope. And Lord for that one that does not feel so royal and chosen because of circumstances, we pray that you will help them to tap into their faith that you have given to them. You have NEVER failed anyone that trusted you Lord. Bring down walls that are standing against your people. You will do it just like you did the Jericho wall. Help them to be quiet, walk in faith, and the wall shall surely fall in Jesus' Name, we thank you!

DECEMBER 12

1 Peter 4:16

But if anyone suffers as a Christian, he is not to be ashamed, but is to glorify God in this name.

DECREE FOR TODAY: We decree that to the righteous good shall be repayed.

Father, in Jesus' Name, thank you for the strength to call upon your Name. Those that call upon you will be delivered. Those that look to you will receive help in the times of trouble. You are sitting on your throne beholding our goings in the earth Lord. We need not worry nor fear. You are our battle-axe. You are our provider. You are all that we need. Thank you for the opportunity to come boldly to your throne to receive help in the time of need! We give you glory for the ability to lift our hands and open our mouths to give you a praise! Hallelujah! For you have given us the garment of praise for the spirit of heaviness. You have delivered us from the powers of darkness and translated us into the kingdom of God. Hallelujah! You will bless the righteous! With favor you will compass the righteous as a shield. In Jesus' Name, we thank you!

DECEMBER 13

Psalm 7:1

O LORD my God, in You I have taken refuge; Save me from all those who pursue me, and deliver me.

DECREE FOR TODAY: We decree that he that feareth the commandment shall be rewarded. We will obey you Lord!

Father, in Jesus' Name, we adore you, Lord. We desire to be filled with knowledge of your wisdom. Give us understanding, Lord. Help us to make wise decisions. Help us to keep our vessels clean, or if we fail to do so, the demons that we were delivered from will return and bring seven other spirits with him. Then we will be worse than we were before you delivered us! We plead the blood of Jesus against everything that tries to hinder our walk. We raise our banners of faith in defense of attitudes in the atmosphere. You are great in us. You are greater than he that is in the world. We will lay hold onto eternal life and let no man take our crown. In Jesus' Name, we thank you Lord!

DECEMBER 14

Proverbs 18:15

An intelligent heart acquires knowledge, and the ear of the wise seeks knowledge.

DECREE FOR TODAY: We decree that if God said it, it shall come to pass. We will look for it!

Father, in Jesus' Name, we will trust in you and do good; with all of our hearts we will trust you Lord, and we will not lean unto our own understanding. How great is your goodness towards those that reverence you. Thank you for allowing mercy to compass us. Thank you for redeeming the souls of your servants. Thank you for making us like Mt. Zion. We shall not be moved by anything. Absolutely nothing can separate us from your love. Thank you for helping us to keep our minds stayed on you. For that, we have perfect peace. In Jesus' Name, we thank you!

DECEMBER 15

Psalm 119:86

All Your commandments are faithful; They have persecuted me with a lie; help me!

DECREE FOR TODAY: We decree that the desire accomplished is sweet to the soul! God will give us the desires of our hearts if we delight ourselves in him!

Father, in Jesus' Name, thank you for giving us the great weapon of faith, which we will use to quench every fiery dart of the wicked. You overshadow us with your care – even knowing the number of hairs that are on our heads. Thank you for valuing us more than sparrows. We will continue to pursue you, Lord, seeking deeper depths and higher heights in you. We will abide in you and allow you to abide in us. We know you will answer our prayers. We are determined to meet you when you return. We are making every effort to be ready, Lord. Thank you for being our hiding place in the chaotic world. In Jesus' Name, we thank you!

DECEMBER 16

Matthew 5:44

But I say to you, love your enemies and pray for those who persecute you.

DECREE FOR TODAY: We decree that a good man leaveth an inheritance to his children's children: and the wealth of the sinner is laid up for the just. God said so!

Father, in Jesus' Name, thank you for your promise that our light affliction is but for a moment. It's working for our good. We are striving to receive our crown of righteousness. You are good and upright. You are a strong hold in the day of trouble. Thank you for the redemption through the blood of Jesus. We are looking through the eyes of faith. We refuse to entertain doubt, negativity and discouragement. We have your promise that you will provide our needs. We have your spirit inside of us to protect us from the powers of darkness. We will use your name JESUS to ward off everything that comes against us. There is power in your Name. Thank you for allowing us to use it! In Jesus' Name, we thank you!

DECEMBER 17

<u>Romans 12:14</u>
Bless those who persecute you; bless and do not curse.

DECREE FOR TODAY: We decree that the righteous eateth to the satisfying of his soul! We shall be filled! No good thing will God withhold from them that walk uprightly!

Father, in Jesus' Name, thank you for your pure word. It is our delight, Lord. Great are your tender mercies towards us. Our hearts stand in awe of your word. Let our supplications come before you. Lord, some are sowing in tears, but you promised that they would reap in joy. Glory to God! You are a helper for those that need strength and a counselor for those that need wisdom. Thank you Lord. In Jesus' Name.

DECEMBER 18

<u>Matthew 5:12</u>
Rejoice and be glad, for your reward in heaven is great; for in the same way they persecuted the prophets who were before you.

DECREE FOR TODAY: We decree that the eyes of the LORD are in every place, beholding the evil and the good. God is watching us! We will not fear!

Father, in Jesus' Name, how great you are, Lord. How mighty and powerful you are. You hung the earth upon nothing. My Lord! Thank you for compassing the waters with boundaries forever. Who can understand the thunder of your power! Nothing, absolutely nothing is hidden from you Lord. Thank you that you miraculously allow prayer to travel around the world, across the oceans, in the prisons, in the hospitals silently but oh God, it brings forth the miraculous! Thank you for getting inside of men's minds to make them do what you want them to do for your people. We give you glory and honor, in Jesus' Name!

DECEMBER 19

Luke 6:23

Be glad in that day and leap for joy, for behold, your reward is great in heaven

DECREE FOR TODAY: We decree that better is little with the fear of the LORD than great treasure and trouble therewith.

Father, in Jesus' Name, thank you for the word of God. If we obey you Lord, we will have peace. We will cling to mercy and truth for then we will find favor and good understanding in your sight as well as man's sight. We will acknowledge you in all of our ways. Then you have promised to direct our paths. We will fear you Lord and depart from evil. We won't be wise in our own eyes. Help us to have sound wisdom and discretion so that we can walk in your way safely and not stumble. We will not be afraid when we lie down; you promised that our sleep will be sweet. We believe it, Lord. We will not be afraid of sudden fear! Our confidence is in you. We thank you Lord, in Jesus' Name!

DECEMBER 20

1 Peter 4:13

But to the degree that you share the sufferings of Christ, keep on rejoicing, so that also at the revelation of His glory you may rejoice with exultation.

DECREE FOR TODAY: We decree that a man hath joy by the answer of his mouth: and a word spoken in due season, how good is it!

Father, in Jesus' Name, thank you that your word declares that the blessings are upon the head of the just; and the just shall live by faith. You said the memory of the just is blessed! Glory to God! Blessings are upon the head of the just: but violence covereth the mouth of the wicked. You have promised that he that walketh urightly walketh surely! Thank you for your protection, Lord. Thank you that you have made us righteous and the mouth of a righteous man is a well of life. Help us to be lights, Lord, and to continue to let them shine. We are epistles read of all men. Bless us to live out your word. Help us to be wise. You have declared that in the lips of him that had understanding, wisdom is found. Thank you for this great gospel, in Jesus' Name!

DECEMBER 21

James 1:2
Consider it all joy, my brethren, when you encounter various trials.

DECREE FOR TODAY: We decree that pride goeth before destruction, and an haughty spirit before a fall. We have crucified pride by the blood of Jesus!

Father, in Jesus' Name, help us to remain humble, to be lowly for that is wisdom. Thank you for delivering the just out of trouble. Help us not to be hypocrites and destroy our neighbors with our mouths. Help us to love one another, even as you have loved us. Help us, Lord, to hold our peace and not be talebearers, revealing secrets. For if our spirit is faithful, we will conceal secret matters. Help us to be gracious. We know that the upright are your delight; help us to continually be upright in your sight, Lord! Whatever we are going through, your word declares that the seed of the righteous shall be delivered! Thank you, Lord God! The desires of the righteous are good. Thank you for answering our prayers and giving us the desires of our hearts, according to your divine will. In Jesus' Name, we thank you!

DECEMBER 22

Acts 5:41
So they went on their way from the presence of the Council, rejoicing that they had been considered worthy to suffer shame for His name.

DECREE FOR TODAY: We decree that understanding is a wellspring of life unto him that hath it. We will get understanding before we make a decision, else it could be detrimental!

Father, in Jesus' Name, we are grateful for everything that you have done for us. Grateful for your provisions. Help us not to complain. Your word declares that better is a handful with quietness than both hands full with travail and vexation of spirit. Thank you for the quietness and peace that you provide for our souls, Lord. We will daily gird up the loins of our minds. We will be alert and hopeful, awaiting your return, Lord. We won't fashion ourselves according to our former lifestyles. But, we will be holy, even as you are holy, Lord. We won't have respect of persons. We will treat all men equally. We will abide in you and in your word; that will guarantee us, Lord, that we can ask anything in your Name according to your divine will, and you will do it. We believe it. We receive it. And, we thank you for it, in Jesus' Name!

DECEMBER 23

Habakkuk 3:17-18

Though the fig tree should not blossom And there be no fruit on the vines, Though the yield of the olive should fail And the fields produce no food, Though the flock should be cut off from the fold And there be no cattle in the stalls, Yet I will exult in the LORD, I will rejoice in the God of my salvation.

DECREE FOR TODAY: We decree that when our ways please the LORD, he maketh even our enemies to be at peace with us - wherever they may be!

Father, in Jesus' Name, we humble ourselves before the mighty hand of God. You will exalt your people in due time. We cast all of our cares upon you. We know you care for us, Lord. We will be wise as far as the adversary is concerned. You have warned us to be sober and vigilant because the devil is as a roaring lion walking around trying to devour whomever he can. We will resist him! We will remain steadfast in the faith. We will make our calling and election sure. We know we are part of your elect, Lord. You have called us out of darkness into your marvelous light. We will walk in it. We won't be deceived. We won't let our children be deceived. We will teach them your word, Lord! You are not slack concerning your promise; you are long-suffering with us, not willing that any of us should perish. Your desire is that we will all come to repentance. Help us to be witnesses for your kingdom, Lord. In Jesus' Name, we thank you!

DECEMBER 24

Romans 5:3

And not only this, but we also exult in our tribulations, knowing that tribulation brings about perseverance.

DECREE FOR TODAY: We decree that hatred is just as powerful

as love. It can be felt many miles away! We will love, even our enemies!

Father, in Jesus' Name, we give you the glory that is due unto your name. We worship you in the beauty of holiness. Your voice is powerful and full of majesty. We adore you, Lord. Thank you for giving strength unto your people and blessing us with peace. Thank you for the power to walk in your might, and to cast down every imagination and high thing that exalteth itself against the knowledge of you, Lord. We appreciate your taking the time to shake each of us this morning and miraculously allow us to wake up. Whatever our state is, we say thank you! Whatever our pains may be, we say thank you for your plans and thoughts towards us are good and not evil and to give us an expected end. Thank you for that guarantee, in Jesus' Name!

DECEMBER 25

Colossians 1:24

Now I rejoice in my sufferings for your sake, and in my flesh I do my share on behalf of His body, which is the church, in filling up what is lacking in Christ's afflictions.

DECREE FOR TODAY: We decree that a man's gift maketh room for him, and bringeth him before great men. We will not be jealous! God has a space for us.

Father, in Jesus' Name, thank you, Lord God, for dwelling in our hearts by faith, so that we can be rooted and grounded in love. Your love passeth all understanding. We want to be filled with all of the fullness of God. We know, Lord, that you are able to do exceeding abundantly above all that we ask or think according to your power that works in us! You give grace to the lowly! You lift up bowed-down heads! You are strength to the weary and the faint. You lift your people to dwell in heavenly places. Glory to God! Thank you for the power not to enter into the path of wickedness but to pass by it and avoid it. Thank you for the Holy Ghost. Help us to attend unto your words for they are life unto those that find them and health unto all flesh. In Jesus' Name, we thank you!

DECEMBER 26

2 Timothy 4:7

I have fought the good fight, I have finished the course, I have kept

the faith.

DECREE FOR TODAY: We decree that death and life are in the power of the tongue: and they that love it shall eat the fruit thereof.

Father, in Jesus' Name, we give you glory and honor for your mighty acts in the earth. You are faithful! You are loving! You are powerful! Lord, we could not endure this life without your hand covering the earth and without the angels that you have dispatched to watch over us. We are grateful. Thank you for every trial and test for they give us patience and understanding. Thank you for every obstacle that has been placed in our paths, for through them we have seen you glory! We bless you, Lord. Your blessings maketh rich and you add no sorry with it. Thank you for being our Comforter. Oh, what a blessing it is to dwell in your presence. Your arms of protection soothe our minds in times of turmoil and dealing with difficult situations. The value of your presence is unmeasurable. Thank you for giving us the opportunity to spend eternity with you. Thank you for the great plans you have for your people. In Jesus' Name, we thank you.

DECEMBER 27

Judges 8:4

Then Gideon and the 300 men who were with him came to the Jordan and crossed over, weary yet pursuing.

DECREE FOR TODAY: We decree that our hope is in Christ. He will never allow the righteous to be shaken! Tell the devil God said so!

Father, in Jesus' Name, thank you for the blood of Jesus that cleanses us from all sins. Oh, what manner of love you have bestowed upon us that we are now called the sons of God. Glory to God in the highest! We know that when you appear, we shall be like you. We have this hope in us. We are grateful that you were manifested to take away our sins. What an honor to be called your child and to receive forgiveness of sins. We know the truth because of you! And if our hearts condemn us, you are greater than our hearts. Thank you for loving us; you are love. Your word says, he that loveth not is not of God. We cannot love you whom we have not seen and hate our brothers whom we have seen. Help us to love as you love, Lord. Help us to speak kind words. In Jesus' Name, we thank you!

DECEMBER 28

1 Corinthians 16:13

Be on the alert, stand firm in the faith, act like men, be strong.

DECREE FOR TODAY: We decree that we will cast our burdens upon the Lord and he will sustain us! It's his word!

Father, in Jesus' Name, thank you for being the Great I AM! We have this confidence in you that if we ask anything in your Name, according to your divine will, you hear us. And if you hear us, we know that whatsoever we ask, you will do it. We will continue to walk in truth. We will follow that which is good. We will shun even the very appearance of evil. Thank you for the power of the Holy Ghost that enables us to walk uprightly. We will earnestly contend for the faith. We will build ourselves up in the faith, praying in the Holy Ghost. You are able to keep us from falling and to present us faultless in your presence, Lord. We will be kind to one another. We will cease from murmuring and complaining. We will trust you to the bitter end, Lord. In Jesus' Name, we thank you!

DECEMBER 29

2 Chronicles 15:7

But you, be strong and do not lose courage, for there is reward for your work.

DECREE FOR TODAY: We decree that just as a father has compassion on his children, so the Lord has compassion on them that fear him! He will not forsake us! It is written!

Father, in Jesus' Name, thank you for comforting us in our tribulations so that we can comfort others which are in trouble, with the same comfort wherewith we ourselves are comforted of you. And, Lord, we know that we may be afflicted or suffer for the salvation of others. Use us to witness. That is our purpose in the earth – to be witnesses for the kingdom. Strengthen us. We will not trust in ourselves, but in you. Thank you for always causing us to triumph in Christ. Thank you for making us a sweet savour of Christ. A royal priesthood! A chosen generation! Glory to God! We are not sufficient of ourselves, but God we recognize that our sufficiency is of you. Thank you for this treasure in earthen vessels so that the excellency of the power is of God, and not us! Sometimes, Lord, we are troubled on every side, yet because of your grace, we are not distressed. Thank you Lord, in Jesus' Name.

DECEMBER 30

<u>Matthew 6:6</u>

But you, when you pray, go into your inner room, close your door and pray to your Father who is in secret, and your Father who sees what is done in secret will reward you.

DECREE FOR TODAY: We decree that we can come boldly to the throne of God and receive help in the time of trouble!

Father, in Jesus' Name, we bless you today! We honor your presence. We pray for the body of Christ that is perplexed, but not in despair. We are persecuted, but we know that you will not forsake us. And we may even be cast down, but because of your grace, we will not be destroyed. Thank you, Lord! We will not faint. Though our outward man perish, our inner man is renewed every day. Lord, you have assured us that our light afflictions, which are but for a moment, are working an exceeding and eternal weight of glory. By faith, we will not focus on the things which are seen. Our faith is in the things which are not seen, which are eternal. Thank you for the promise to create a new heaven and a new earth, where there will be no more crying, no more dying, no more pain! Glory to God! Thank you that when this earthly tabernacle is dissolved, you have a building waiting for us, a house not made with hands but eternal in the heavens. In Jesus' Name, we thank you!

DECEMBER 31

<u>Hebrews 13:15</u>

Through Him then, let us continually offer up a sacrifice of praise to God, that is, the fruit of lips that give thanks to His name.

DECREE FOR TODAY: We decree that better is the ending of a thing than the beginning! Better is Coming!

Father, in Jesus' Name, that you for bringing us to the close of another year, and to the close of this prayer book. We pray that souls have been touched. We pray that your people's minds and hearts have been blessed through reading this book. We pray that your people have been strengthened and encouraged. We pray that as we close out another chapter in each of our lives, that we are stronger, that we are more determined to be ready to meet you when you return, and that we will keep our focus on you, Our Blessed Hope! Thank you for this journey of faith, Lord! You have been faithful. We are still here. We pray that each of us will use this day to give you glory, to encourage others, and to maintain our walk with you, Lord. Thank you, Lord! In Jesus' Name!

Books by Helen Alexander

A Daily Word From God

Sunday School Lessons

Daily Prayers

Rapture Ready

Made in the USA
Charleston, SC
26 September 2016